THE ARTS OF SPAIN

THE

with 62 colour plates and 100 black and white plates

ARTS OF SPAIN

JOSÉ GUDIOL

THAMES AND HUDSON
LONDON

This edition © Thames and Hudson 1964

CONTENTS

Preface

This book is intended to bring the reader closer to a world of art that is much less familiar than it should be, to a country rich in legend and history, and to a culture that was for centuries a bridge between the Atlantic and Mediterranean civilizations.

What is fascinating about Spain is that although it speaks one language, it has many voices. Its unity derives from its very old civilization and art and is based on national temperament; its variety derives from its location between Europe, Africa and the Americas, from foreign invasions, changing modes and the evolution of ideas.

It is to be hoped that this book will contribute to a better understanding of a country that has been a steppingstone between three continents and the cradle, especially as far as Spanish America is concerned, of vigorous regional arts often superior to the original. Nor has the influence come to an end. Picasso and Miró, famous throughout the world, epitomize the continuing vitality of the Spanish force in art.

JOSÉ GUDIOL RICART

Barcelona, 1964

Chapter I

The Age of Invasions

THE GENIUS OF PREHISTORIC ART

The prehistoric paintings of the Iberian Peninsula have their origin in magic and religion. They are sometimes found on blocks of stone, but more often in caves and rock shelters, where daylight penetrates feebly if at all. As materials, the artist used mineral pigments mixed with fat or oil; the texture is that of a true oil painting. Often the work was incised in the rock, and in some cases the natural roughness of the cave walls was used to achieve a three-dimensional effect.

Spanish rock paintings can be divided according to style into three main groups occurring in three periods. The first is believed to have coincided with the Upper Paleolithic, ending somewhere between 20,000 and 8,000 B.C. The art of this period is characterized by the predominance of the animal form, either in motion or in repose, but always majestic and usually standing free. The best work in this early style can be seen in the Altamira caves (Plate 1) near the Cantabrian city of Santander. The impression created by the life-sized figures of bison, horses, wild boars and other animals, shown grazing, running, leaping, with head turned and in an endless variety of natural poses, is one of prodigious realism. The only colors used are black, red, and yellow ocher, and a few mixed pigments. There is an evident appreciation of differences in pictorial concept, inasmuch as the striking linearity of some figures is contrasted with a rendering of masses and a true modeling in others. Figures which must belong to different epochs of the Magdalenian period are often found side by side. However, paintings from the same epoch have been discovered in other parts of Spain, specifically in the Pileta cave (Málaga) and in a cave at Saelices (Guadalajara). In the latter there is an impressive engraving of the head of a wild horse of the Aurignacian period.

It would be making a serious mistake to assume that the only value of these paintings lies in their antiquity. Many of them are inspired works of art, revealing talent comparable to that of the greatest artists of the historic period. They may be regarded as celebrations of the life force. What the sensitive observer misses, perhaps, is the feeling for composition and the organization of space that was gradually to emerge in the art of later periods.

The second group of paintings appears to correspond in time with the Mesolithic period, beginning near the end of the Upper Paleolithic, and lasting roughly from 10,000 to 3,000 B.C. The novel element in

1   Standing Bison. Prehistoric painting in the Altamira Cave (Santander)

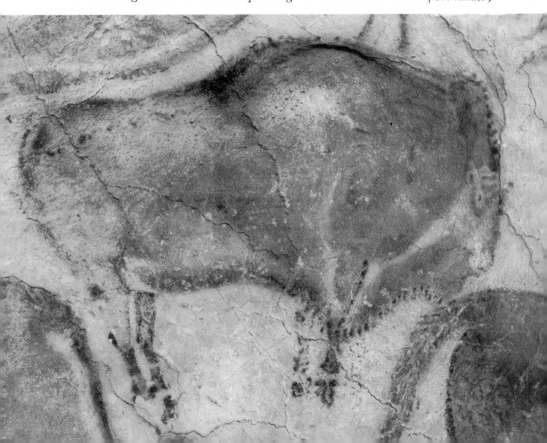

2 Hunting Scene. Prehistoric painting in the Remigia Cave, Ares del Maestre (Castellón de la Plana)

these paintings is the use of true composition. The figures of animals are now joined by the human form, which is given full value. The earlier naturalism is modified by a tendency toward the schematic, appropriate in a portrayal of action.

The walls of the Remigia cave at Ares del Maestre in the neighborhood of Castellón de la Plana are covered with dynamic images of hunters, bulls, wild goats and other animals, but more important than the individual figures is the scene itself. An extraordinary unity of rhythm is apparent in every composition (Plate 2). The swiftness of movement is cleverly rendered by simplifying the figures and concentrating more on gesture than on form. Important paintings are also located in rock shelters at Cogul, Alpera, Calapatá, and other places, mostly in the Mediterranean foothills.

The cave paintings of the third and last group belong to the Neolithic, which spans the last three or four thousand years before our own era. In style they are highly schematic. Figures often become

3 Prehistoric idol from Andalusia. Prats Collection, Barcelona

mere signs and there is a marked interest in ideological concepts. The forms of men and animals are reduced to a few simple lines. The emphasis has shifted from the naturalistic but lively narrative of the artists of eastern Spain to other scenes of a cosmic nature. Idols and symbols representing the sun and perhaps the stars mingle with the most varied schematic interpretations of the figures of men and animals. Characteristic is a triangular diagram for the body, and, for the face a pair of dots standing for eyes. The same features are found in the slablike or cylindrical idols that constitute the first known sculptured images of prehistoric Spain (Plate 3).

Neolithic improvements in toolmaking during the Mesolithic period stimulated the development of architecture. Its earliest manifestations appear to have been ritual, funerary, and religious in nature, including menhirs, dolmens, and large structures complete with passageways and spacious chambers. The latter were built with enormous slabs of stone, some with dome-like roofs. A number of these chambers are found in different parts of Andalusia, the famous Menga cave in Málaga being an outstanding example. This architecture belongs to the second and third millenniums B.C. and is related to subsequent Iberian and Celt-Iberian work contemporaneous with Roman domination of the area.

THE ROLE OF MEDITERRANEAN TRADERS

Toward the end of the prehistoric period, the Iberian Peninsula was populated by Iberians and Celts. In the central regions these races mingled to form the Celt-Iberian people. The culture of these restless, warlike tribes must have been very much the same as that of other parts of Western Europe. Its most important material expressions, known to us today, are metalwork in bronze and iron, pottery and walled villages. The level of civilization was raised by the arrival of various peoples from the East who established colonies at points along the coast suitable as trading posts and as ports of call for vessels following the tin route. The strangers brought with them the alphabet and the arts, exerting a strong influence on the Iberian tribes and stimulating their latent artistic talents.

The Phoenicians founded Gádir (Cádiz) about 1,000 B.C.; the Carthaginians started a colony at Ebusus (Iviza) in 654 B.C.; and one hundred years later the Greeks came to Rosas and Ampurias (Gerona). The only example of Phoenician sculpture in Spain is the anthropomorphic sarcophagus in the Museum of Cádiz (Plate 4). This dates from the fifth century B.C. and is modeled on Greek work. The baked clay figurines found in the Carthaginian necropolis on Iviza form a remarkably interesting collection of great iconographic variety and genuine artistic merit. Pottery, glassware, and jewelry, like that which forms part of the Aliseda treasure in the province of Cáceres, complete our brief review of Phoenician art in the Iberian Peninsula.

The Greek finds reveal the importance of the maritime colony of Ampurias. Prominent among the sculpture is a marble statue of Aesculapius in the archaic tradition. Stone, bronze, and baked clay

4 *Anthropomorphic sarcophagus from Cádiz. Phoenician sculpture. Museum, Cádiz*

figurines and pieces of decorated earthenware, glass, and ivory have been found in relatively large numbers. Greek terra cottas, jewels, and weapons, notably the Jávea treasure (Alicante), have also turned up in other parts of Spain. Most of the objects found were probably imported, but some, like the sphinx of Agost (Alicante), are clearly Iberian works of art fashioned under Greek influence.

BALEARIC CULTURE

During the millennium preceding the Christian era, a distinctive Bronze Age culture developed on the islands of Majorca and Minorca. The center of development was probably the peninsular area of Los Millares–El Argar (Almeria). The greatest achievements of the Balearic culture are its Cyclopean structures: *talayots*, or cylindrical watchtowers, forming part of the defenses of fortified settlements; *navetas*, buildings with a rectangular plan and slanting walls, the most notable example of which is the *naveta* of Tudons (Minorca); and

5 *Bull's Head from Costitx (Majorca). Balearic sculpture. Bronze. National Archaeological Museum, Madrid*

taules, consisting of a smooth slab of stone raised vertically to support another slab laid horizontally. The *taules* probably served for laying out the dead or as places of worship. Some interesting settlements, like that of Capocorp Vell in Lluchmayor (Majorca), have also been preserved, together with subterranean sepulchers, walled enclosures, and çave dwellings. As for the minor arts of the Balearic culture, there remain only pottery, weapons, belt clasps, necklaces, and certain other objects. Among these the great heads of bulls found in Costitx (Majorca) are unique (Plate 5). Cast in bronze, they may be derived from Celto-Mycenaean art, although they are much more recent than the work of that civilization. Many small bronze images of bulls and doves that were probably votive figures, have also been found.

IBERIAN ART

Chronologically, the origins of Iberian art are somewhat vague, though they definitely belong to the last one thousand years B.C.

Iberian work undoubtedly possesses a certain unity, due largely to its Mediterranean character, so different from the ornamentalism of the Celts and Teutons. There is clear evidence of Greek and Carthaginian influence, and possibly even an echo of the mysterious culture of Tartessus, the biblical Tarshish.

Iberian art did not embrace the whole peninsula, but spread over broad areas of eastern Spain at the same time as the Greeks and Carthaginians were establishing their Mediterranean colonies. The architectural remains are confined to habitations, necropolises, and burial chambers. These were generally built in Cyclopean masonry, but sometimes the stone was carefully dressed, as in the burial chamber at Tugia (Jaén). Certain decorative architectural elements are definitely original, though stylistically related to the Mediterranean cultures. The decoration is limited to geometric patterns, lightly incised, and to broad, interlacing curves, carved in relief.

Sculpture and metalwork in gold are the most conspicuous features of Iberian art. Its outstanding achievement, the Lady of Elche (The Prado), is a gray limestone bust, carved in the middle of the fifth century B. C., and still bearing traces of polychromy (Plate 6). The finely modeled features display an expression that is somewhat abstracted, but nobly severe.

The Lady of Elche is one of the world's finest pieces of sculpture, and, of course, a masterpiece of the archaic period that preceded the classical age of Greece and Rome. The Greek or Carthaginian influence is felt more as a stimulus to the artist than as an actual borrowing of style. The originality of this work lies in its spirit as well as in its form, and in its fusion of the austere and the baroque, in which the eternal qualities of the Spanish temperament are already joined.

More Iberian stone sculpture has been found at Cerro de los Santos (Albacete). The fact that many stone effigies, both standing and sitting, numerous heads, and busts were discovered in this area strongly suggests that they are votive figures from some major sanctuary. The iconography and style are equally interesting. Flowing robes, headdresses, and jewels are represented in a formula that is

6   *The Lady of Elche. Iberian sculpture. Polychrome stone. The Prado, Madrid*

marked by geometric folds and lends rigidity to the figures, emphasizing the plastic value of the masses. Figures of animals, sometimes with human heads, are also common in Iberian art. An excellent example is the *bicha* ("animal figure") of Balazote, a perfectly proportioned and subtly stylized bull with the head of a man. This review of Iberian stone sculpture, brief as it is, would be incomplete without a reference to the reliefs from Osuna (National Archaeological Museum, Madrid), which must have been decorative elements in some large building. They depict soldiers, horsemen, and women in procession. A romantic scene with two heads face to face is particularly charming. The style of these reliefs indicates that Iberian sculpture was influenced in its last period by Roman art.

Iberian art also produced large numbers of exquisite small bronzes, used as votive offerings. Some of these, representing persons of both sexes, variously clad, and animals, are naturalistic, while others are reduced to little more than stick figures. The finest examples are

7 *Decoration on an Iberian vase from Liria. Archaeological Museum, Valencia*

distinguished by an aesthetic stylization which gives the essence of both form and gesture. This quality is apparent in two small figures found at Despeñaperros (Jaén), one a warrior with sword and shield, the other a woman wrapped in a loose cloak that descends to her feet. Certain Iberian sanctuaries have yielded as many as 2,500 small pieces of this kind.

The burial chamber at Galera (Granada) shows that mural painting must have existed during the Iberian period. Some idea of the drawing and sense of representation of the Iberians can be obtained from their pottery. The designs are a synthesis of schematic, decorative, often highly stylized elements, and a spirit of realism. No large and sumptuous pieces have been found, only a varied collection of household pots, especially water vessels. Ovoid, spherical, cylindrical, and bell-shaped forms alternate with others subtle enough to bear comparison with Greek ceramic ware, although without the latter's formalism.

These vessels, variously decorated and painted with red ocher, obviously reflect a popular taste. The decorative motifs are usually geometric, with stylized fauna and flora. Concentric waves, parallel lines, and rhythmic spirals are combined with simple flowers and leaves or birds with outstretched wings—like those on urns from the necropolis at Archena (Murcia)—all traced with great delicacy. Sometimes the artist portrayed a procession of soldiers or an actual scene with people dancing or playing games. The style may lean toward a certain expressionism which adds intensity and even occasionally spontaneous humor to the outlines of the faces. Some compositions, like those on vessels from the Iberian city of Liria (Archaeological Museum, Valencia), depict animated movement in a manner that is almost cinematographic (Plate 7). Horsemen and foot soldiers brandish spears, oarsmen row, and transparent fishes swim about, their backbones made visible in accordance with primitive tradition. Huts, houses, and forts are more sketchily indicated. Vase painting was rather late in maturing, reaching its high point somewhere between the second century B.C. and the first century of our era.

The remainder of Iberian art consists of silver-damascened weapons and clasps and jewelry in precious metals. This art is now regarded more as an independent aspect of Mediterranean culture than as merely the product of parallel influences. There can be no doubt that the Iberian element per se is more important than any of the alien forces that may have conditioned it or stimulated its development. This is confirmed by the accompanying illustration (Plate 7), which, though it gives some idea of the beauty of certain specimens of Iberian art, cannot communicate their strength and originality. It is necessary to visit the admirable collection of the National Archaeological Museum in Madrid to realize that the Spain of the last five centuries B.C. was indeed a source of work of universal interest.

The Celtic Wave

The Celts entered Spain from the North in two successive waves, the first arriving about 700 B.C., the second some two centuries later. Evidence of their influence has been found from Catalonia to León and Portugal. The only pieces of monumental Celtic sculpture that still remain are the great stone statues of warriors (Guimarães, Portugal) and animals, including the famous Guisando Bulls in Avila (Plate 8). We also have a few steles with narrative reliefs, more related to the art of Northern Europe. Skillful metalworkers, the Celts also left us weapons remarkable for their beauty of form and fine ornamental workmanship, such as the damascened swords from the necropolis at Las Cogotas (Avila) and torques and necklaces found in Galicia. Uniting with the Iberians, they formed the Celt-Iberian nation, a people jealous of their independence and tenaciously resistant to Roman domination. Excavations have brought to light some crude furniture that indicates a rather primitive way of life, yet the pottery is decorated with stylized figures of surprising vitality.

THE ROMANIZATION OF IBERIA

The Romans gradually extended their unifying influence throughout the length and breadth of the Mediterranean. In 218 B.C. the invasion of Spain by Scipio inaugurated a long and bitter struggle that continued until A.D. 19, the year marking the end of Augustus' war against the Cantabrians. Under the Romans the separate sources of Hispanic culture merged and Latin civilization was grafted onto the native tradition, already refined by contact with Carthaginians and Greeks. The Romans left their mark on Spain in the form of impressive works of architecture and engineering. Using their unique system of construction, based on stone masonry, the arch, and the vault, they built walls, triumphal arches, temples, forts, bridges and aqueducts, theaters, arenas, and commemorative and funerary monuments. They covered the Iberian Peninsula with a network of paved roads, linking it with Rome by way of Gaul. Sculpture, mosaics, bronzes, pottery, glassware, weapons, and jewelry testify to the richness and unity of this civilization nourished both by Etruria and by the diffusion of Hellenistic culture.

The principal qualities of Roman architecture are strength and harmony. These are in full evidence in the structures erected in the Spanish provinces, which are characterized by a certain simplicity compared with the buildings of the capital. Among the Roman

bridges, two of the finest are the bridge over the Guadiana river at Mérida, built in the time of Augustus, and that over the Tormes at Salamanca. Both of these, however, are surpassed in grandeur and beauty by the bridge at Alcántara (Cáceres), dedicated to Trajan, the center pillar of which reaches a height of almost 158 feet. A small shrine at the entrance to the bridge commemorates the Roman builder, who, in an inscription, proudly proclaimed that his work would "last as long as the earth herself." The structure was completed in A.D. 106. The great aqueducts are almost a symbol of Imperial Rome. The most important one in Spain is that at Segovia, a massive granite structure over 90 feet high and almost 2,400 feet long (Plate 9).

A number of Spanish cities still preserve their Roman walls, some of which are monumental in appearance. These walls were usually built of stone and mortar and dotted with square or round towers. The monumental walls of Tarragona, said to have been built by Scipio, are perhaps the best preserved, though the walls of Barcelona,

8 (Left) Bulls in Gui-
sando (Avila). Celtic sculpture. Stone

9 (Right) Roman aque-
duct in Segovia

dating from the third century, and those of such places as Lugo and
Carmona are also well worth mentioning. The temples, market places
and forums have not fared so well. All that remains of the great
temples at Mérida and Tarragona is a few columns and other frag-
ments. Among the funerary monuments, the tomb of the Attilios at
Sádaba is remarkable for its harmonious complexity and the so-called
tomb of the Scipios, near Tarragona, for its striking simplicity.
Monumental arches of a commemorative nature still stand at Cáparra
(Cáceres), Bará (Tarragona), Mérida (Badajoz), and at Medinaceli
(Soria).

The finest of the eighteen theaters the Romans built in Spain is
that at Mérida, erected at the order of Agrippa and completed in
18 B.C. The stage is framed by two tiers of twenty-eight Corinthian
columns with marble statues set between them. Among the best preserved amphitheaters are those at Itálica, Mérida, and Tarragona.
The palace of Augustus at Tarragona, a spacious building in solid

10   The Sacrifice of Iphigenia. Roman mosaic in Ampurias (Gerona)

stone, gives some idea of Spanish domestic architecture during the Roman period. Similarly, excavations in villages and towns and the remains of villas unearthed in the richer agricultural regions of the Iberian Peninsula indicate that the methods of construction and decoration were typical of those employed throughout the Roman Empire.

Spain is very rich in Roman mosaics. They have been found *in situ,* covering the floors of great country villas and important urban buildings. These include the splendid Sacrifice of Iphigenia found at Ampurias, the Medusa at Tarragona, and many other interesting examples with mythological or narrative themes (Plate 10). Among the latter we should mention the chariot-racing scenes in the circus (Museum, Barcelona).

The Roman sculpture found in Spain is varied in both subject matter and style. The most common finds are busts, evidently of important people, some of whom have been identified, and statues of the gods. The older works reflect the Hellenistic tendencies that prevailed in Rome during the second and part of the third centuries B.C. Though never entirely lost, these tendencies later gradually gave way to the sterner taste of Roman realism. In some pieces both these influences are combined, whereas others bear the mark of the long period of decadence that began in the second century A.D.

Most of the work of better quality must have been imported from Rome herself, although this does not exclude the possibility that Hispano-Roman studios existed too. Among the more outstanding pieces in the Hellenistic style are the marble Dionysos, found at Tarragona, the Pomona, sadly incomplete, from the same city, the marble Venus of Itálica, and the torso of Hercules, found at Valladolid, a realistic portrayal of an athlete of the period. Statues like that of Pluto in Mérida or that of Ceres, which stood in the theater of the same city, are in a style more characteristically Roman. But the Roman artist's fidelity to nature is even more apparent in busts, a type, indeed, created by Rome. In spite of the idealization of certain heads, particularly those of some of the emperors, there can be no doubt of the artist's real interest in the personality of his model, betrayed in the sharp differentiation of the features. This is true of a number of heads of Augustus found in various parts of Spain, including the bronze head from Azaila and those in marble from Itálica and Mérida that perfectly express the majesty of the founder of the Empire.

Not only the emperors are portrayed with the force and naturalness of truth; citizens and senators, girls and matrons, all live on in marble. Their features are reproduced in a style that seizes upon the essentials and combines energy with a convincing tactile quality. Certain heads, like the bronze head of a woman, found in Ampurias, appear somewhat archaic and stylized, but the majority are genuine portraits of real human beings. To this latter group belong the effigies recently recovered from excavations around the walls of Barcelona, the magnificent bust of Valladolid, and many other marbles found in Seville, Cordova, Mérida, and Tarragona (Plate 11).

Funerary sculpture is well represented in Hispano-Roman art, as witnessed by a variety of elaborately carved marble sarcophagi. The

11 (Left) Roman portrait bust. Marble. Archaeological Museum, Barcelona

12 (Right) Early Christian sepulchre mosaic. Early Christian Museum, Tarragona

virtuosity of the sculptors is evident in the flexibility of the rhythms and the skill with which they blended the many different figures and elements of the design. While on the subject of Hispano-Roman sculpture, we should not omit mention of the admirable friezes, capitals, altars, plaques, cornices, columns, and other decorative architectural fragments, found in abundance in many of the cities of Spain.

Roman art has often been accused of being formal and "official," but in the provinces, as in Spain, it is prone to reveal its human side. The problems of the beyond, family sentiment, the idea of the motherland, and a universal order find expression in the artistic forms and lend them nobility. As for the great engineering works, they testify to a lively and constant interest in the progressive establishment of a civilized order

Early Christian Art

The Early Christian art of Spain represents the final stage of Roman influence. The cultural exchange of the first few centuries A.D. was soon threatened by the incursions of the Germanic tribes, which began in the year A.D. 409.

Santa Eulalia de Bóveda (Lugo), a subterranean building with a basilican plan, and the unusual domed structure at Centcelles (Tarragona), decorated with mosaics and frescoes of great interest, are among the few noteworthy architectural relics of this period.

Sculpture is represented mainly by ornamented sarcophagi. The symbols of the chrismon (monogram of Christ), the crown of victory, and strigils (a series of S-shaped flutings) alternate with illustrations of incidents from the Bible and allegorical scenes. Some of this work is certainly Spanish, for example, the sarcophagus of Leocadius at Tarragona, in which the Roman style has been refined into what is obviously an anticipation of the Romanesque.

Some free-standing sculpture, including a number of versions of the Good Shepherd, has also been found, together with mosaics that follow Roman models in conception, technique, and color sense. Outstanding among the latter are those at Centcelles, already mentioned, and the sepulchre mosaic dedicated to Optimus, found in the necropolis at Tarragona (Plate 12). Here the deceased is depicted in strong lines, the mantle falls in sober folds, and the features are expressive. The figure, correctly proportioned, stands out against a floral background.

THE VISIGOTHS

The Germanic invasions of the fifth century and the conquest of Spain by Islam in A.D. 711 were episodes in the final decline of the ancient world. The great destruction wrought by incessant wars and the limited cultural baggage of the races descending from the North are reflected in the scarcity of monuments surviving from this period. Something of the Roman style remains, but increasingly modified by alien influences.

13   San Pedro de la Nave (Zamora). Visigothic architecture. Seventh century

In the development of the new art, North African tendencies were balanced by the conversion of the Spanish Visigoths to the Church of Rome and their admiration for classical civilization. The North African influence was felt in architecture, the decorative carving, and pottery, whereas the minor arts, particularly metalwork, have a style of distinctly Nordic, that is, of Celto-Germanic, origin.

In order to appreciate the beauty of Visigothic art, it is necessary to pay attention to detail and recognize the life that breathes in its abstract shapes and rhythms. Moreover, metalwork, the general category of most of what has been preserved, imposes certain rules that suited the temperament of the Germanic tribes. The Visigothic, however, is characterized by a degree of humanization derived from close contact with the Latin mind. Here we can already perceive the origins of the synthesis of barbaric and classical art, which, after a long period of gestation, was to culminate in the Romanesque.

The rise of Visigothic architecture is marked by several fine churches. One is the church of San Juan de Baños (Palencia), built by King Reccesvinthus in 661; it has three rectangular apses and three aisles separated by columns supporting the horseshoe arches which were typical of Visigothic architecture. The capitals are of stylized floral design, remarkable for the vigorous handling of the masses. The greatest architectural achievement of the period is San Pedro de la Nave, near Zamora, a work of the last third of the seventh century. Cruciform in plan and vaulted, it is distinguished by its spatial harmony and superb masonry. The sculptural decoration is richer and more highly evolved than in the earlier buildings of the Visigoths. The capitals are well-composed and the undulating surfaces of the cymatia (crowning moldings) are adorned with figures of animals and with floral scrolls (Plate 13). This is a singular style that creates a very flat low relief with contours defined by sharp ridges.

The church of Quintanilla de las Viñas in the province of Burgos is the last of the more ambitious works of the period. It is remarkable for its wall carvings. The exterior of the church is enlivened by broad friezes depicting birds and floral motifs. Inside there are four bas-reliefs of unusual symbolic interest. The arches are also decorated, with themes similar to those of the façade.

In metalwork the Spanish Visigoths produced a wealth of belt

14 Gold Crown of King Reccesvinthus. From the Visigothic treasury at Guarrazar. Seventh century. National Archaeological Museum, Madrid

clasps and brooches encrusted with precious metals and glass. The masterpieces of the goldsmiths' craft of this period, with its taste for rude magnificence, are the splendid votive crowns of the treasury of Guarrazar, near Toledo, and the crosses that accompany or adorn them (National Archaeological Museum, Madrid, and Musée de Cluny, Paris). These crowns are gold, set with precious stones and rock crystal, and hung with beads, metal links and letters spelling out the king's name. In one instance (Plate 14) twenty-two pendant letters make up the words RECCESVINTHUS REX OFFERET (King Reccesvinthus offered it). Other concentrations of the art of the Spanish Visigoths have also come to light, notably the treasure found in the Cordovan town of Torredonjimeno (Museums of Cordova, Madrid, and Barcelona).

Chapter II

Orient in Occident

The Moslem invasion began in A.D. 711 with the incursions of Tariq and Musa and soon established their rule throughout the Iberian Peninsula, except for a few scattered centers of resistance in the north, from which the reconquest was eventually to come. It was not until the thirteenth century, however, that the Christians regained control of most of Spain.

There were various reasons for the completeness of the success of the Moors: aid from the Jews and treachery from within, but above all the general indifference of the people to the presence of the conquerors. Ever since the fifth century the Hispano-Roman population had lived in subjection to Visigothic lords with whom they had nothing in common. The victory of the Moors merely substituted one set of rulers for another.

Like their predecessors, the Moors were interested in keeping alive the productive forces of the country in order that their feudal system, with its ruling warrior caste, might be sustained by the labors of peasants and artisans. On the whole, the Christians were well treated. They kept their own laws, clergy, and religion, and even held certain civil offices. The ties between conqueror and conquered were further strengthened by frequent intermarriage between Spaniards and Moors and Berbers, who were only thirty-seven thousand strong when they first occupied Spain.

Doubtless, the level of religious tolerance did fluctuate somewhat, depending on the temperament of the ruler and local conditions. Islam preached against the bonds of servitude; to obtain his freedom a subject had only to embrace the faith. Thus there was formed, by legal means, a large body of Mohammedanized Christians, living side by side with those more obstinate in their attachment to ancient customs and traditions. This accounts for Mozarabic art and its diffusion toward the north of Spain, through the vast regions that suffered the endless struggles between different cultures and religions.

HISPANO-MORESQUE ART AND CIVILIZATION

The Arabs, essentially a nomadic people, readily assimilated the cultural influences to which they were exposed either by conquest or by other forms of contact. Thus, the culture of Islam was largely compounded of Greek science and strong elements of Byzantine, Syrian, and Persian art, the whole governed by religious fanaticism. These borrowings, however, reappeared in new and original forms, characterized by a tendency to repetition, a unique feeling for the infinite, manifestations of which are apparent in Islamic ornamentalism and architecture.

The mosque, or house of prayer, is always built to face Mecca, but is not designed for any true religious ceremony. An essential feature of the interior is the *mihrab*, a Mecca-oriented prayer niche in the wall facing Mecca. The minaret is a slender tower from which the muezzin calls the faithful to prayer. The *sahn*, or forecourt, of the mosque always contains a *sabil*, or fountain, for the ablutions that the faithful must perform before entering the sacred precincts.

Sculpture in the round and painting in the sense of figure composition are rare in Islamic art. Nevertheless, it cannot be said that Islam absolutely forbids the representation of plants and animals or even the human form.

Ornamentation is rightly regarded as one of the greater glories of Islamic art. Surfaces are covered with unbroken lines that twist and undulate in elaborate geometric patterns; the same patterns are found on many architectural elements in the form of *almocarabes* (vault decoration) and ornamental plasterwork. One must bear in mind the traditionalism of Islamic art, which was quick to assimilate and impose

15   *The Mosque of Cordova. Hispano-Moresque architecture. Tenth century*

its unity on concepts and techniques of the most diverse origin. Thus, for example, the horseshoe arch, used by the Spanish Visigoths, became a basic element of Hispano-Moresque architecture. The Mesopotamian techniques for carved stucco and glazed pottery, used with such effect in the art of Eastern Islam, experienced an extraordinarily vigorous development in Spain.

Before proceeding to an examination of its monuments, we should point out that Hispano-Moresque art differs from that of the East in possessing a certain "classical" quality which has been hailed by art historians as one of Islam's valuable acquisitions from the West. Simplicity of form, of course, is clothed in the most sumptuous decoration, and surfaces are transformed to suggest a world of fantasy, identical in spirit with the art of Damascus and Baghdad.

In the Arabic scale of values, as opposed to the classical, it is the applied arts that take precedence, while ornamentation ranks higher than form. Art, it is felt, should be at the service of life, not the reverse. In all this there is a sense of the ephemeral, an eagerness to surround oneself with beauty rather than to create a beauty that is itself eternal. The reasons are doubtless to be found in climate and in the history of the race. Nevertheless, there were certain aspects of Greek and Roman culture that the Arabs did appreciate and succeeded in assimilating.

The Mosque of Cordova

This is the most important monument of Hispano-Moresque architecture (Plate 15). The original mosque, built under Abd-er-Rahman I during the years 780–787, was a square, somber, fortress-like structure with buttressed front walls. The interior, 250 feet long and 246 feet wide, was divided into two roughly equal parts—the mosque proper and the *sahn* or forecourt. The roof was supported on 142 columns, all recovered from Roman or Visigothic sites. From these columns spring pink and white double arches, alternately brick and stone. Additions by successive rulers have increased its length by 150 feet.

16   The Mihrab *of the Mosque of Cordova. Hispano-Moresque architecture. Tenth century*

The new construction follows the scheme of the old. The columns, which have no base, are alternately black and pink with capitals of stylized and simplified Corinthian type, carved by the masons of the caliph. The new extension consisted essentially of the upper end with its festooned cusped arches and the *mihrab* chapel (Plate 16). The friezes, pilasters, and arches are profusely decorated with floral, geometric, and calligraphic motifs. The animation of the interlacing cusped arches enhances the sense of an art based on fantasy. Hakam asked the Byzantine Emperor Nicephorus to send him a skilled mosaicist to decorate the *mihrab* chapel. This part of the mosque, which is reserved for the devotions of the emir, and the two areas flanking the *mihrab* are roofed with cupolas formed by intersecting vaults. The front and interior of the *mihrab* are covered with Moorish plaster work of dazzling richness, while its arches and cupola are embellished with mosaics. The various decorative panels are carved in marble and stucco.

17 Arch in the Aljafería Palace, Saragossa. Hispano-Moresque architecture. Eleventh century

The last additions to the mosque were made by al-Mansur, the vizier of Hisham II, the work continuing until 987. Eight new aisles, running the entire length of the building, were added on the east. The style of the arches is a simplified version of Hakam's work.

Apart from the Mosque of Cordova, the greatest architectural achievement of the tenth century was the construction of Medina az-Zahra, near Cordova. Among the ruins one can still discern the double wall, clusters of buildings, and the sites of palaces with decorative elements of the finest quality, the true culmination of Islamic ornamental sculpture. Construction began under Abd-er-Rahman III in 936; work on the project continued until 976. The chroniclers and geographers who visited the city at the height of its magnificence give identical accounts of its splendors: glass mosaics from Byzantium, marbles from Greece, Carthage, and Rome, ivory doors richly carved, decorative sculpture in gilded metals, blazing with precious stones. The little that remains is still enough to inspire belief in these descriptions; the richly carved walls, pavements, and capitals, adorned with stylized foliage, are work of great beauty.

THE TAIFAS

After the death of al-Mansur, the Caliphate of Cordova dissolved into a number of *taifas,* or small, independent kingdoms. In some instances this resulted in the infusion of new vigor and cultural vitality into the towns that became the capitals of these petty states. One of these was Toledo, which soon regained the prestige it had formerly enjoyed under the Visigoths and embarked on a period of expansion and development that was to last for several centuries. Its mixed population of Moslems, Christians, Jews, and Mozarabs gave Toledo a special cosmopolitan character, which it retained even after the reconquest by Christians in 1085. We have relics of the caliphate in the

Overleaf 18:

"The Witches" textile. Hispano-Moresque. Twelfth century. Archaeological and Artistic Museum, Vich (Barcelona)

19 Leyre Coffer. Hispano-Moresque sculpture. 1005. Ivory. Cathedral of Pamplona

Bisagra Gate with its horseshoe arch, and in the mosque of Cristo de la Luz, completed in 999 and inspired by the Byzantine churches of Constantinople during the Comnenus dynasty. This building is square in plan and has Visigothic capitals. It is distinguished by the variety of the vaulting.

On the whole, the city that acquired most power under the taifas system was Saragossa. Between 1039 and 1081 the Beni-Hud dynasty built the magnificent Aljafería palace, which, though often mutilated, still stands (Plate 17). The arches, carvings, cornices, capitals, and other structural and decorative elements make this building one of the finest examples of Islamic art.

MINOR ARTS OF THE FIRST HISPANO-MORESQUE PERIOD

We have already noted that Islamic sculpture is primarily decorative. Nevertheless, certain reliefs, dating from the ninth to eleventh centuries, do depict animals and even human beings. Some are to be found on marble basins from the time of the caliphs, especially one from Seville decorated with the figures of birds and animals, including eagles, and lions attacking stags. This basin, used for ablutions, bears the name of al-Mansur, who ordered it for his palace at Azzahira in 987. The eleventh-century basin of Játiva is remarkable for its representations of the human form, carved in miniature style.

Although classified as sumptuary art because of its small size and function, Moorish ivory carving has considerable sculptural value. A number of pieces from the workshops of the caliphs have fortunately been preserved. Among them is the lovely casket (dated 964) from Zamora cathedral, now in the Archaeological Museum in Madrid. The coffer of Fitero (966) is signed by an artist called Halaf, who also carved a casket now in the Louvre (968) and a third piece owned by the Hispanic Society in New York. The casket of Braga cathedral (Portugal) and the Leyre coffer in Pamplona cathedral (Plate 19), both carved in 1005, are other examples of superb craftsmanship. The iconography of these carvings is based on the use of medallions enclosing human forms, set against an elaborate background of floral work, stylized animals, and other decorative motifs.

In the decorative arts the Moors achieved a high level of refinement and beauty, particularly in ceramics, an art concerning which they learned a great deal from the potters of Mesopotamia and Persia. Whereas the ceramic ware of medieval Europe was of extremely poor quality, the Moors of Spain produced some astonishingly fine work, which was exported everywhere, from France to Constantinople. It is characterized by a variety of form, the quality of the glazing, a limited color range, and the imaginative and lively rhythms of the decoration. The glazed pottery from Elvira (Granada) in white, green, and violet, decorated with the figures of men and animals and ornamental motifs, probably dates from the ninth or tenth century. Even greater importance was achieved by the "golden" lusterware, which must have been produced in the caliph's workshops during the tenth century. In style this Hispano-Moresque ware is similar to later work from centers such as Rhages, Susa, and Fostat. Advances in technique led to the production of the first pieces in molded relief. This method was successfully employed by the Málaga potteries during the eleventh and twelfth centuries and marked the transition to a more avowedly decorative phase. The ruins of the caliphate centers, as Medina az-Zahra, Bobastro and Málaga have also yielded examples of bright yellow ware known as *cuerda seca* (dry cords) faïence.

The Moslems' skill in casting metals is displayed in their censers, lamps, mortars, and braziers. Many of their stylized animal figures, like the bronze stag in the Cordova Museum and the Monzón lion in the Louvre, are genuine works of art. Unfortunately, only one worthy example of the craft of the silversmith has survived from the days of the caliphs. This is the casket in Gerona cathedral, which Hakam II had made for his son Hisham about the year 970. Miscellaneous pieces of gold and silver jewelry show how beautiful the work of the Moorish craftsman could be.

A few fabrics, embroideries, and tapestries of the period have also been preserved, mainly in the form of shrouds or the linings of reliquaries from Christian Spain, which always valued the products of the regions under Moslem influence. A reliquary in the church of San Isidoro at León has an embroidered lining that probably dates from the beginning of the eleventh century. The Museum of Vich (Barcelona) has a fine Hispano-Moresque textile called "The Witches" (Plate 18).

THE PURITANISM OF ALMOHADE ART

The spirit of the Almohade sect was puritanical and ascetic. Its founder, ibn-Tumart, was a theologian. His dynasty reigned over North Africa and part of Spain between the middle of the twelfth century and the year 1269. The Almohades, essentially a hill people from the Atlas

20   *The Giralda Tower, Seville. Almohade architecture. Twelfth century*

44

Mountains, landed in Algeciras in 1151. Cordova and Carmona surrendered and elsewhere resistance was generally slight. The tendency of the Almohades to make their mosques and public buildings as simple and austere as possible finds a clear parallel in the Christian religious movement started by St. Bernard, which championed Cistercian art. At the same time, the Almohades were anxious to prove themselves worthy successors to the caliphs. In architecture, however, they accomplished little, and, unlike the Cordovan dynasty they did not use materials of a quality equal to the grandeur of their designs. Mud and brick were substituted for stone, plaster for marble and granite. Ornamentation was sparingly used. Where formerly there had been a lavish profusion of reliefs, there was now a little cautious decoration surrounded by broad areas of bare surface. It is interesting to note that Almohade architecture and decorative motifs penetrated the military frontiers of Christendom, their influence being reflected, with perfect stylistic orthodoxy, in certain monuments of Toledo and Burgos. The Almohades also developed the art of fortification well in advance of the peoples of Europe.

The finest achievement of the Spanish Almohades was the great Mosque of Seville, which must have been built, according to contemporary evidence, between 1172 and 1182. Among the elements of the original structure that have been preserved are the beautiful Court of the Oranges and its magnificent minaret, the famous Giralda, a square tower completed around 1195 (Plate 20). The façades were decorated with carved brick and with pointed, cusped arches above double windows.

Seville possesses another noble example of Almohade architecture, the Alcazar, a citadel of imposing towers and walls, with a court, the Patio del Yeso, noted for its lovely arcades and its carved stuccoes, some of which later served as models for the Nasrid Alhambra.

Christian Spain has several works of typical Almohade architecture that reveal the attraction exerted by Islam on the Castilian kings. The royal monastery of Las Huelgas at Burgos, founded by Alfonso VIII in 1187, contains a chapel, the Capilla de las Claustrillas, built in the first quarter of the thirteenth century in pure Almohade style. The presbytery has a cupola supported on squinches. The free use of cusped, mixtilinear, and segmental arches gives character to the design.

Another example of Almohade architecture is Santa Maria la Blanca in Toledo, a former synagogue remodeled about 1250. The decorative stucco, a dense tissue of fine lines, is limited to well-defined surfaces and specific elements, and contrasts sharply with the smooth whiteness of walls, columns, and arches.

During the Almohade period the applied arts continued in the earlier tradition. The *almimbar* or Moslem pulpit preserved in the mosque of the Kutubiyya in Marrakesh (Morocco), a piece of Cordovan workmanship from the middle of the twelfth century, bears witness to the skill of the wood carvers and inlay workers of that time. Examples of bone inlay are afforded by various caskets preserved in the Cathedral of Tortosa (Tarragona) and in Madrid's Archaeological Museum. They are decorated with the stylized figures of animals and men and calligraphic forms. The bronze Puerta del Perdón (Door of Pardon) in Seville cathedral is a fine specimen of the art of embossed metalwork. In ceramics, the familiar lusterware continued to be produced. As far as textiles are concerned, most of what has been preserved comes from Christian tombs. Some especially fine remnants are kept in the monastery of Las Huelgas at Burgos, in particular the banner of Las Navas de Tolosa, a silk tapestry with Koranic texts, figures of lions, and a starred polygon.

The history of Almohade art is that of the gradual surrender of the rough African conquerors to the delights of the aesthetic attitude to life that prevailed in Andalusia. The same period was also remarkable for its flourishing poetry, which, together with the more refined applied arts, prompted a cult of pleasure that did much to soften the harshness of the Koran. The continuing victories of the Christian kings over Spanish Islam, particularly after the loss of Toledo (1085), may have contributed to the growing sensualism of Hispano-Moresque art and to that atmosphere of somewhat artificial refinement that persisted from the Almohade period down to the final years of the Kingdom of Granada.

NASRID ART

In the second quarter of the thirteenth century Mohammed I founded the Kingdom of Granada, which lasted until 1491, when the capital was finally taken by the Catholic kings, a defeat that marked the end of Moorish power in Spain. Between 1236 and 1248 Ferdinand III reconquered Cordova, Jaén, and Seville. Many craftsmen sought refuge in Granada, rather than make their way to Morocco. This helps to explain the richness of Granadan or, as it is called, Nasrid art, which developed vigorously along independent lines for a century and a half and then drifted on in languid decadence for a century more.

Whereas earlier Moorish society in Spain had remained in active cultural contact with the East, Nasrid civilization lived in seclusion within its own boundries. The Granadans accorded architectural decoration and importance equal to, if not greater than, that it had enjoyed in the time of the caliphs. Mostly they built palaces, showing a strong preference for shut-in effects and the fragmentation of space. Their villas and gardens were always designed with a full complement of fountains, basins, or pools. On the other hand, their concern for durability grew progressively less, and a certain degeneracy inspired them to erect buildings that were as luxurious in appearance as they were flimsy in construction. Nevertheless, certain fortifications show that the feeling for solid workmanship had not been entirely lost.

Traditional decoration was further enriched by the use of tile marquetry for socles and floors, while picturesque polychromy was applied to stuccowork and even marble capitals. Arches and vaults were adorned with "stalactites," a form of ornamentation recalling the roofs of limestone caves. Calligraphic, geometric, and floral motifs were all employed and tended to merge. Ceramics, rich fabrics, ivories, and the products of the goldsmiths and other craftsmen were actively exported to Christian lands.

It is possible to detect a certain parallel between the evolution of Arabic art and the evolution of the Christian art of the West. There is, so to speak, a Hispano-Moresque Romanesque and a Hispano-Moresque Gothic. There must have been a constant interplay of cultural influences between the Christian kingdoms and the kingdoms of the Moors, though, in general, purity of style was not affected. On

21   *Court of the Lions in the Alhambra, Granada. Nasrid architecture. Four-teenth century*

the other hand, the spirit that underlies the forms reveals either a parallel evolution or, at least, the acceptance of certain tendencies. Thus, the art of the Kingdom of Granada was finally to merge with the Gothic in the Flamboyant and Mudejar styles, creating hybrid forms of great majesty and beauty that express the mingling of two races and the fusion of two spirits. An example of this can be seen in the interior decoration of the Infantado ducal palace in Guadalajara.

The Alhambra

Occupying a roughly rectangular site on a hill in Granada, the Al-hambra, the palace of the Moorish kings, consists of an irregular group of buildings surrounded by a wall flanked with towers. Most of these buildings are in a truly remarkable state of preservation, thanks chiefly to the concern of the Catholic kings and their successors. Work on the Alhambra was begun by Mohammed I in 1238. Like much Moorish construction, the final complex is the result of juxta-posing a series of independent units, without any predetermined plan. A forecourt, the ruins of the royal mosque, and the Machuca court and tower are earlier than the Mexuar (1365), where the king received his subjects. The tower of Comares, built by Yusuf I (1333–1354) and more than 140 feet high, is crowned by the Hall of the Ambas-sadors, the largest room in the palace, remarkable for its cedar dome, arches, and carved stucco. Beside it is the court of Comares, completed in 1369 and famous for the harmony of its broad rectangular pool and its north and south arcades. In the direction of the wall there follow, in succession, the royal baths, the tower called the Peinador de la Reina (the queen's dressing room), the gardens and *mirador* of Daraxa, and the Hall of the Two Sisters, all beautifully decorated. The Hall of the Two Sisters gives onto the Court of the Lions, one of the masterpieces of Nasrid art; rectangular in plan, it is surrounded on all four sides by galleries supported on 124 slender marble col-umns (Plate 21). This court dates from the reign of Mohammed V (1354–1391). This complex of beautifully decorated buildings is sur-rounded by gardens and secondary structures, which in turn are en-closed by the great ramparts and the Alcazaba, a citadel planted on the crown of the hill. The reddish color of these impressive fortifications harmonizes with the luxuriant green of the Granadan flower gardens.

The kings of Granada had other palaces, towers, and gardens in the city. The most interesting of these is the Generalife, a summer palace completed by a series of groves and gardens embellished with pools and fountains. Pre-eminent among Granadan public buildings is the so-called Corral del Carbón which served as market and hostelry. Monumental in proportions, it has a beautiful porch and a large central court with three galleries supported by pilasters.

Nasrid Applied Arts

Ibn-Khaldun, an Arab historian of the second half of the fourteenth century, states that the Nasrids adopted the Christian custom of decorating their houses with representations of the human form. To this we owe the interesting narrative paintings that adorn three cupolas in the Alhambra's Hall of the Kings, and those of the Casita del

22   Alhambra   Vase.   Nasrid art.   Fourteenth   century.   Museum   of   the   Alhambra

Partal, with their small figures of horsemen, hunters, and soldiers. As for sculpture, apart from the lions grouped around the famous Alhambra fountain, it was mostly confined to reliefs, decorative panels, and ivories.

Ceramics, woodwork, carved stucco, and marble reliefs were lavishly employed in Nasrid architecture, but the same craftsmen also turned their talents to producing household goods of equal beauty. The art of ceramics, in particular, was stimulated by the constant use of lustered tiles, particularly for wainscoting and floors, but sometimes even for vaulted ceilings. Moreover, from the thirteenth century tiles had also served to decorate the exteriors of buildings. One of the finest examples of Nasrid architectural ceramics is the so-called Fortuny tile panel (Instituto Valencia de don Juan, Madrid), discovered in a house in Albaicín (Granada). Remarkable pieces of lusterware continued to be produced, among them a number of large vessels—up to 66 inches tall—such as the magnificent Alhambra vase, made of reddish clay decorated in gold and blue, with gazelles confronting each other around the top (Plate 22). Málaga was the chief center for this earthenware, much of which was exported.

Nasrid ivories are less crowded with reliefs than those of the caliphate. The Instituto Valencia de don Juan and the Museum of Vich (Barcelona) have some fine caskets, while the Madrid Army Museum has the carved hilts of the famous swords of Boabdil and Aliatar; the workmanship of the pommels speaks highly for the skill of the Granadan metalworkers. Woodwork is well represented by some exquisitely inlaid fourteenth-century cabinet doors in the Alhambra Museum, and metalwork by the magnificent lamp of the Alhambra mosque in the National Archaeological Museum in Madrid. This lamp, which, according to an inscription around its edge, dates from 1305, is in cast bronze, fretted, and embossed. The textile industries flourished under Nasrid rule, particularly the silk industry, which was centered in Murcia, Almería, and Málaga. Carpets were widely used. They had been woven in Moorish workshops since the time of the Almohades, and, according to the arab geographer al-Idrisi, they were being made in Murcia early in the twelfth century. Granada was also known for its artistic leatherwork, the leather being first tanned and then embossed, gilded, and variously colored.

Chapter III

The Middle Ages

THE MOZARABS

The art of the Mozarabs, that is, of Christians who lived under Islamic rule, embraced much of northern and central Spain, the chief center being León. It arose toward the end of the eighth century and reached its greatest heights during the two centuries that followed. In certain forms it persisted into the twelfth century and had an important influence on Spanish Romanesque.

Mozarabic art found its fullest expression in architecture, where it is characterized by a preference for the horseshoe arch and the basilican, or cruciform, plan. The buildings of the Mozarabs are embellished with decorative elements such as capitals, friezes, and fretted panels. The carving is obviously influenced by Islamic taste, but there is plenty of evidence of the old Visigothic tradition with its typically Nordic associations. Mozarabic churches are generally small, the exteriors simple, with little or no decoration. Brick and stone are used either independently or in various combinations.

Apart from architecture, the greatest strength of Mozarabic art lies in its illuminated manuscripts; in fact, many designs and color formulas of these miniaturists reappear in the early Romanesque.

A few ivories, bronzes, and pieces of embossed silver have been preserved, but not in sufficient quantity for us to be able to trace the evolution of style in the minor arts.

The region of Spain where Mozarabic art is mostly found was much afflicted by the terrible struggle between Christians and Moors, changing hands frequently as the advantage passed now to the one side, now to the other. Though the long struggle for the reconquest of Spain was undoubtedly punctuated by certain periods of relatively peaceful coexistence, at times the intolerance was utterly merciless, and in the long run most Mozarabic architecture was destroyed.

In the southern half of Spain, dominated by the Arabs until the thirteenth century, only two Mozarabic buildings survive. One, the little church of Bobastro, in the mountains not far from Málaga, was built in 898–917 and has three aisles separated by rows of columns

23 *San Miguel de Escalada (León). Mozarabic architecture. Tenth century*

and horseshoe-shaped arches, and Santa Maria of Melque, near Toledo, which has a cruciform plan and resembles a castle.

By the year 900 Mozarabic culture expanded right across Spain, from Asturias and Galicia all the way to Catalonia. In Asturias, Mozarabic influence was often confined to decorative elements, super-imposed on structures built in the Ramiran style. Catalonia has several interesting churches dating from this period: the basilica of San Miguel de Cuixá in Roussillon, consecrated in 974, is big and bare; San Quirce

24 San Baudel de Berlanga (Soria). Mozarabic architecture. Tenth century

de Pedret, with its horseshoe-shaped apses, is known for its paintings and Santa Maria de Marquet for its elaborate horseshoe arches.

Mozarabic art experienced its most vigorous development in the Kingdom of León, doubtless because León was at the head of the struggle to drive out the Moors. Two boldly conceived basilicas of noble proportions, both built about the same time, attract immediate attention. These are San Miguel de Escalada (Plate 23) and San Cebrián de Mazote. The former has a high nave, traversed by an arcade with three horseshoe arches, and two aisles. An arcaded porch, added in 921, enhances its charm. Both churches have a series of beautiful Corinthian capitals—some taken from earlier buildings. Moreover, in both churches the characteristic corbels of the roof reveal the influence of Cordova. The other churches of the region form a distinctly homogeneous group. A striking example of Mozarabic architecture in Castile is San Baudel de Berlanga (Plate 24).

Mozarabic illuminated manuscripts, one of the supreme achievements of the Spanish art, have their roots in the Caliphate of Cordova, although other Eastern and Nordic influences are discernible. The tenth-century Hispalensis Bible (or Sevillian Bible), with its quill drawings of horseshoe arches and emblematic figures, is clearly inspired by Cordova. The *Commentary on the Apocalypse* by Beatus of Liébana, written about 786, was a much-copied manuscript that remained an inspiration to miniaturists until well into the thirteenth century. The most important copy, that from the monastery of San Miguel de Escalada, was completed in 926 and illustrated by the painter Maius (Morgan Library, New York). Inspired by Byzantine miniatures, Magio nevertheless developed a style of his own, which was to be widely imitated (Plate 25). In his old age, Magio also illuminated the Távara Beatus. In Magio's art the figurative elements of reality are represented schematically and its sharp expressiveness is heightened by the clever use of color.

The art of the Mozarabic miniaturists, so impressive in its strength and beauty, is well exemplified in other copies of the Beatus manu-

25   Page of the Beatus from San Miguel de Escalada (León). 926. Pierpont Morgan Library, New York

frandoruma faccatu̇ quum ABeia

nubuquodonoror Incumpo uram

ubinubuquodonoror prefgia
saltuc misac & ubinucgo
miacure Infornuce

script, notably that of Valcavado, that of Urgel, and that of the Cathedral of Gerona, completed in 975; the profuse illustrations of the latter are signed by a woman artist *Ende pintrix*.

As for the minor arts, little of these from the troubled Mozarabic period has survived. Nevertheless, we must not omit to mention two fine tenth-century ivories, the cross in the Louvre, and a portable altar, both from San Millán de la Cogolla. In addition, there is the silver altar of San Pedro de Roda, with its stylized *repoussé* designs, and the cross of Santiago de Peñalba (Museum, León).

THE ASTURIAN KINGDOM

The struggle against the Moslem invader began in Asturias, which rapidly developed into an important cultural center, closely followed

26 (Facing) Naranco Palace, Oviedo. Asturian architecture. Built by Ramiro I (842–850)

27 Gilded coffer given by Alfonso III (886–910) to the Cathedral of Astorga (León). Asturian art

by Carolingian Catalonia. Asturian art, which includes work of great significance, falls naturally into three periods. The first of these is well represented by the crypt of the Cámara Santa of Oviedo cathedral and by the church of San Julián de los Prados, probably built between 812 and 842. The latter is a large church with three vaulted aisles decorated with mural paintings of the kind that must have covered the interior of all the Asturian churches. The motifs are ornamental, representations of buildings and draperies in the Pompeian tradition, but with a character of their own derived from late Roman work. The dominant colors are gray-blue, red and yellow ocher.

Asturian art reached its peak during the second of its three phases, that corresponding to the reign of Ramiro I (842–850). Three buildings from this period have rightly been described as unique. These are the Naranco Palace (Plate 26), San Miguel de Lillo, and Santa Cristina de Lena. They are decorated with sculpture and mural paintings wrought in a style betraying both Northern and Eastern influences. The unusual circular shields that decorate both the inside and the outside of the Naranco Palace are particularly interesting. San Miguel de Lillo has some handsome stone grillwork and some finely carved door jambs decorated with circus scenes in a very flat and schematic style. A pilaster in the same church shows three scenes with figures vertically superposed, a device that recalls Irish art of the same period. An interesting feature of Santa Cristina de Lena is the altar iconostasis (screen), although this is later work, doubtless of the tenth century.

During the third period, the solemnity and grandeur characteristic of earlier Asturian art and its refined ornamentation fell prey to a certain decadence. Nevertheless, this period did yield one building of importance, the church of San Salvador de Valdediós, consecrated in 893. The same type of architecture was employed in popular Asturian churches from the ninth to the eleventh centuries.

The achievements of Asturian art are by no means confined to its architecture and sculptural decoration. The work of the goldsmith is represented by a number of pieces of the highest quality, like the Cross of the Angels, from the early part of the ninth century (Oviedo cathedral), adorned with uncut rubies and antique stones set in gold filigree. The enameled Cross of Victory, a more intricate design, was commissioned by King Alfonso III early in the tenth century. The gilded and *repoussé* Coffer of the Relics in Astorga cathedral (Plate 27) and the Coffer of the Agates that Fruela II gave to the Cathedral of Oviedo in 910 also date from this period.

Although Asturias was the focal point of Christian activity in the Iberian Peninsula during the ninth century, Catalonia, which had been reconquered by Charlemagne, formed the important Spanish March, the southern line of defense of the Frankish Empire. There is a group of three Carolingian churches in Tarrasa (Barcelona) that deserves mention for unusual structural interest.

ROMANESQUE ART

In Europe the eleventh century was a period of intense building activity. The social and political climate was favorable. Spiritual unity had been achieved as a result of the imposition of the authority of the pope, and the monastic orders, especially the Benedictines of Cluny,

28 San Clemente de Tahull (Lérida). Romanesque architecture. Church consecrated in 1123

29   Lintel dated *1021* at *St.-Genis-des-Fontaines* (*Roussillon*)

30   (*Facing*) *Portico of San Isidoro at León. Romanesque architecture.*
1054–1067

were deeply engaged in their civilizing task. Cathedrals, churches and
monasteries, castles, and fortifications were rising everywhere. The
Pilgrimage roads, linking one religious center with another, were organized to a remarkable degree.

From all this activity there emerged a new architectural style, the
Romanesque, which, though composed of many diverse elements, gave
convincing expression to the spiritual unity that had inspired it. The
wide diffusion and ready acceptance of Romanesque art are attributable, at least in part, to the nomadic character of the medieval craftsman. Not only individual sculptors, builders, and mural painters, but
whole bands of artisans wandered far and wide in search of work. This
tended to stimulate, rather than impede, the establishment of workshops attached to monasteries and cathedrals.

In spite of its universality the Romanesque style did not prevent
the development of a number of national schools with a certain measure of stylistic independence. The Spanish version of Romanesque
is distinguished mainly by its expressive qualities. In general, it lacks
the refinement of the French schools and the classical associations of
Italian Romanesque. Sculpture and painting are infused with a rather
strange expressionism, apparently derived from popular art, in which
human and religious sentiment prevails over purely aesthetic emotions
and considerations of form. A basis of tradition, handed down from
early antiquity and modified by Byzantine influences, already existed

in Spain. The impression left by the Carolingian and Germanic cultures was less strong. In the south, Eastern characteristics, transmitted by the Mozarabs, played a part in determining certain features of the Spanish Romanesque. In fact, it is important to remember that in Spain the Romanesque period coincided with the most critical phase of the struggle to oust the Moslem invader, led by the kings of Aragon and Castile. The outcome of this struggle was not finally decided in favor of the Christians until the middle of the thirteenth century, by which time the Gothic style had begun to emerge and the Moors were confined to a limited area in the south, centered in the Kingdom of Granada.

The most characteristic qualities of the Spanish Romanesque, in its purest form, are austerity and strength. The strength is that of its Roman and Byzantine heritage, which finally succeeded in imposing its discipline on primitive and Eastern elements alike. Essentially a religious art, it established, in its iconography and in its architecture, a hierarchy corresponding to its own conception of the world.

Romanesque architecture finds its highest expression in its churches. These are generally either in basilican or cruciform plan, though in some instances the two forms are successfully combined. Sculpture and painting are employed both to decorate the structure and to instruct the faithful in the truths of their faith. The portals are adorned with statues and reliefs, which in some cases extend over the entire façade; at the same time, sculptural decoration is applied to numerous other structural elements, inside and outside the church.

Early Romanesque Architecture and Sculpture

The earliest Romanesque architecture, dating from before the year 1000, is found in the region of the Pyrenees. Some of these buildings reveal Carolingian influence, others Mozarabic, while in a third group both influences are fused. The great monastery of San Pedro de Roda, in the heart of a landscape that now evokes a semilegendary world, must be included in the latter category. Its sculptural decorations are stylistically related to those of St.-Genis-des-Fontaines and St.-André-de-Sorède in Roussillon. This suggests the existence of a regional school of stonecutters, since the same manner is noticeable in different localities. Typical of their style is a handsome lintel, carved in 1021, in the church of St.-Genis (Plate 29). The figures, in low relief, are sharply incised; the intention appears to have been more ornamental than strictly representational. Christ, enthroned, is shown in a mandola supported by two angels with outspread wings. The large letters of the inscription form part of the design, which is firmly contained within a vigorous floral border. There is a similar lintel in St.-André-de-Sorède.

The Lombard style, characterized, in decoration, by the use of blind arcades, and, in construction, by the use of rubble masonry, was introduced into Catalonia in the time of the famous Bishop Oliva (died 1046). The churches have one or three aisles with continuous barrel vaults and a semicircular apse, very simple porches, and tall bell towers with twin windows. Perhaps the first church of this type, in Catalonia, is Santa Maria de Rosas, which was consecrated in 1022. The older parts of Santa Maria de Ripoll (1032), San Clemente de Tahull (Plate 28), and many other buildings of the Pyrenees belong in this style.

In spite of the advantages of the Lombard system, in the eleventh century structures of dressed stone continued to be built in Roussillon and the region of Gerona. Among them are Ste.-Marie of Arles (1046) and Elne Cathedral, and, on the south side of the Pyrenees, San Pedro de Galligans, Besalú, and Porqueras, churches dating from the latter part of the century. The style of the sculpture is fairly primitive, but full of strength, and already displays that imagination in the juxtaposition of figures and forms that was to become one of the characteristics of Romanesque art.

During the eleventh century Aragon and Navarre shared a common architectural style. In these two Pyrenean kingdoms the early Romanesque is represented by a number of small churches and by the monastery of Leyre. The magnificent sanctuary of the latter is a structure of the utmost monumentality, the decoration rude, but full of grandeur.

In the western part of the Iberian Peninsula, the Romanesque style was slower to emerge. It was the middle of the eleventh century before it finally imposed itself upon Visigothic-Asturian tradition and Mozarabic taste. A masterpiece of this early phase of the Romanesque is the portico of San Isidoro in León, built between 1054 and 1067 as a royal burial place, at the instigation of the king, Ferdinand I

(Plate 30). In this portico a noble sense of space is allied with structural and decorative elements of extraordinary strength. Short, thick, vigorously functional columns support groined and domed vaults. For originality and variety of carving, the heavy capitals are among the finest of the Spanish Romanesque. Some employ the motifs of Moorish plasterwork, others depict floral patterns and animal heads, or figures enacting sacred and allegorical scenes. Monsters, face to face, and real and legendary animals offer a pretext for powerful plastic effects. In the groups of human figures every detail has been deliberately stylized, for the sake of general unity. A century later the impressiveness of the architecture and carving was further heightened by a series of ceiling paintings, to which we shall refer again. The church to which the portico belongs was rebuilt toward the end of the eleventh century.

In Spain the last quarter of the eleventh century saw the evolution of forces that were to contribute to the general renewal and unification of Romanesque architecture and sculpture. Stylistically, the new movement was eclectic, drawing freely from a number of different European schools; geographically, it extended over the entire length of the pilgrim route to Santiago de Compostela. These buildings are large, structurally refined and, handsomely carved. The Cathedral of Jaca possesses a unity of style that reflects the personality of a great artist. The so-called Master of Jaca carved the tympanum of the west portal and the capitals, some with nude figures of great naturalism and beauty. The classicism of his style suggests contact with Italian sources.

The castle of Loarre, the greatest Spanish fortress of the Romanesque period, has certain affinities with the Jaca school. In the crypt of its chapel, begun about 1071, there are capitals obviously derived from those of the Master of Jaca.

About 1100 a number of very talented sculptors were at work in Aragon, among them the Master of Doña Sancha, named for the princess whose tomb he carved. Navarre, which had many ties with Aragon, has numerous churches that can be regarded as links in the chain of style along the great Northern pilgrim route.

31 Relief, cloister of Santo Domingo de Silos (Burgos). Romanesque sculpture. Eleventh century. Stone

Continuing toward the west, in Palencia we find another remarkable example of the influence of Toulouse and Jaca. This is the church of San Martín de Frómista, built about 1070. The columns of its three aisles and windows support numerous well-designed capitals. Architecturally, it is a work of great purity of style and structural perfection, and it may be regarded as the first Castilian masterpiece of the Romanesque.

Still farther to the west we find the church of San Isidoro de León, built by Petrus Deustamben to replace the older structure that once occupied the same site. Until 1200 the new church served as a model of the Romanesque in León. The reliefs over the main door are remarkable for their formal intensity. The south door of the transept is also decorated with carvings.

In Santiago de Compostela the art of the pilgrim route reaches its climax. The cathedral, begun in 1075 by the architect Bernardo the Elder, was completed by the master builders Estebán and Bernardo the Younger. Superior carving is evident in the decoration of the apse, but the most interesting and varied work is to be found in the transept, above all in the so-called Platerias door, completed early in the twelfth century. Both door and façade are adorned with a profusion of sculptures and reliefs, evidently by a number of different hands. Great refinement alternates with simple competence and laborious craftsmanship. Nevertheless, viewed as a whole, this is one of the most important examples of Romanesque sculpture in Europe.

In the province of Burgos there are a number of buildings equal in age to those along the pilgrim route, but wholly independent in style. In fact, their decorative elements reveal a distinctly Eastern influence, no doubt introduced by Islamic craftsmen. Two such buildings are the monastery of Oña and that of San Pedro de Arlanza with capitals and imposts of Moorish origin. More important, for the sake of its sculpture, is the monastery of Santo Domingo de Silos, founded in 1041. The original church no longer exists. The cloister was begun in the last quarter of the eleventh century. A number of sculptors shared in the work, the most gifted being the one who carved the many highly original capitals and the magnificent reliefs that adorn the piers (Plate 31). This artist has rightly been named the Master of Silos. Judging by his style, he was probably a Moslem, since his compositions are suffused with the spirituality of an orientalism adapted to the plastic idiom of Western art. The sacred figures are grouped in a conventional, rather archaic manner and all the available space is filled in order to achieve harmonious rhythms, reinforced by repetition of gesture. He is sensitive to the values of his surfaces, which he models with refinement, and is not afraid to go beyond mere stereotyped characterization. All these scenes, with human and animal figures and tiny buildings, are framed by arches beneath a checkered abacus. The capitals, carved with the figures of animals trapped in nets and stylized flowers, are also sculptural elements of more than ordinary interest. In some parts of the building, the Door of the Virgins, for example, the capitals, though related to the rest, are more advanced in style.

The Twelfth and Thirteenth Centuries

From about 1125 uniformity, which had been widespread (though neither systematic nor complete) and which had derived from proximity to the pilgrim route to Santiago de Compostela, gave way to a desire for change. In Catalonia and Castile, and the regions in between, local schools of architecture and sculpture began to achieve some degree of independence. Under the influence of these new trends, the models of the international Romanesque underwent certain modifications, leading in some instances to a return to archaism—which has been responsible for not a few errors in dating.

One of the foremost schools of the twelfth century, with a reputation that extended throughout the Pyrenees, was that of the region of Roussillon, the style of which has special affinities with the sculpture of Ripoll and Vich. In this part of the north, the link between the eleventh century and the magnificent flowering of the decorative arts in the twelfth is to be found in the cloister of Cuxa (The Cloisters, New York). In this cloister all the decorative elements are carved in pink or white, gray-veined Pyrenean marble (Plate 32). Doubtless, the marble quarries of Roussillon supported a flourishing school of sculptors whose work was widely exported.

The most important achievement of the Roussillon marble carvers is probably the decoration added, in about 1151, to the church at Serrabona. This consisted of a porticoed gallery and choir in the

32 (Left) Cloister from St.-Michel-de Cuxa (Roussillon). Eleventh century. The Cloisters, Metropolitan Museum of Art, New York

33 (Right) The miraculous Fishing. Relief from San Pedro de Roda (Gerona). Twelfth century. Marble. Marés Museum, Barcelona

central aisle and additional work on the façade. The Master of Serrabona had the skill to infuse new vitality into well-worn formulas. The porch of St.-Michel-de-Cuxa, the church of Cornellá de Conflent, the cloister of Elne cathedral, and various other buildings have decorative elements that reveal the influence of the Roussillon group.

In the monastery of Santa Maria de Ripoll there still stands a magnificent portal, from the second quarter of the twelfth century. The jambs, archivolts, and surfaces of this splendid portal, which has a single opening and no tympanum, are covered with a series of iconographic reliefs, possibly derived from the famous Bible of Ripoll, and dominated by the figure of Christ. These reliefs are inspired by passages from the Gospels and the Old Testament, and by incidents involving historical personages, like the Abbot Oliva, who intervened decisively in the life of the monastery. The design as a whole is extraordinarily well conceived, particularly with respect to the relation-

UBI DNS AIT UT DISCIPLIS IN MARI

PAX
NO
BIS

ship between the height of the relief and the proportions of the figures, which vary in size depending on their position within the general plan. The palms and intertwining flowers are the principal ornamental motifs. Ripoll is also noted for its cloister with capitals of Pyrenean marble.

The most forceful personality among the many craftsmen who linked Roussillon with Catalonia and other areas of the north was undoubtedly the anonymous sculptor known only as the Master of Cabestany, whose art is remarkable for its expressionism. The wanderings of this artist can be traced from Errondo in the Pyrenean region of Navarre through various points in the south of France to Catalonia, where he carved the main porch of San Pedro de Roda (Plate 33).

Throughout the second half of the twelfth century Catalonia went on building churches and monasteries, most of them with cloisters. This important element of medieval religious life, with its low, easily visible, and varied capitals and good illumination, is an excellent example of architecture and sculpture harmoniously related. Often the iconography of the capitals follows lines laid down by abbots and bishops, in conformity with sacred, narrative, or allegorical themes. Romanesque cloisters vary conspicuously in scale, from the small, almost intimate proportions of San Pedro de Galligans in Gerona, completed about 1154, to the boldness of Gerona cathedral and the monastery of San Cugat del Vallés, where the cloisters correspond to the final phase in the evolution of the type and must belong to the last quarter of the twelfth century.

In Catalonia Romanesque architecture and monumental sculpture end with the building of the great cathedrals of Lérida and Tarragona. By this time the thirteenth century had already begun and the influence of Cistercian simplicity was strong.

During the twelfth century, Aragon and Navarre continued to share a common style. Navarre produced a number of interesting masters. This school evolved slowly and persisted into the thirteenth century.

34 Allegorical composition. Fresco from San Quirce de Pedret (Barcelona). Twelfth century. Museum, Solsona

35 *Cloister of San Juan de Duero (Soria). Twelfth century*

During the second half of the twelfth century Castile was the scene of much building activity. Castilian art of this period is eclectic, more interesting in its decorative than in its structural aspects. In Santander, its most outstanding achievements are the churches of Cervatos, Castañeda, and Santillana del Mar. The latter has a sanctuary inspired by that of San Isidoro in León. It also possesses a fine cloister with delightful capitals of a primitive kind.

In Burgos there is some exceptional carving in the later parts of the cloister of Silos. A similar style is evident in the monastery of Las Huelgas and other monuments of the region.

Logroño, Soria, and Segovia are remarkable for the frequent use of porticoed galleries in the churches, a type of construction that is also found further south. The cloister of San Juan de Duero (Plate 35), an important monument built under Moorish influence, is very reminiscent of Sicilian work in Amalfi and Palermo. Arabic elements are also apparent in the decoration of various other porticoed churches of Segovia.

*36 Old Cathedral of Sala-
manca. Twelfth century*

Certain connections with the Segovian style are to be found in Avila, but, as the twelfth century advanced, there followed a strong influx of ideas from central France, doubtless due to the arrival of numbers of artists from that area. One of the finer churches of the city is San Vicente, with its magnificently carved porches. San Vicente also houses the monumental tomb of SS. Vincent, Sabina, and Cristeta.

During the second half of the twelfth century a number of important buildings were erected in León. These buildings are richly carved and share a number of common stylistic features, characterized by a certain Eastern influence, which may have found its way through the Poitou along the pilgrim routes. The Cathedral of Zamora, built

Overleaf 37:

The Virgin and St. Bartholomew. Fresco from San Clemente de Tahull (Lérida). c. 1123. Museum of Ancient Art, Barcelona

75

38 (Left) Master Mateo. Pórtico de la Gloria, Cathedral of Santiago de Compostela (Coruña). 1168 to 1217

39 (Right) Two Apostles. Sculpture in the Cámara Santa, Cathedral of Oviedo. Twelfth century. Stone

Overleaf 40 and 41:

(Left) Master of Pedret. St. John. Fresco from San Pedro del Burgal (Lérida). Eleventh century. Museum of Ancient Art, Barcelona. (Right) Master of Maderuelo. Fresco from the apse of Santa Maria de Tahull (Lérida). Twelfth century. Museum of Ancient Art, Barcelona

between 1151 and 1174, has pointed arches in all aisles, indicating an evolution toward the Cistercian style. Its most characteristic element, however, is its superb cupola, which bears a resemblance to certain Syrian domes.

The magnificent collegiate church of Toro, begun in 1160 and completed one hundred years later, is plainly related to the Cathedral of Zamora. It, too, has a cupola and large windows decorated with scrollwork. The carving of the north porch is particularly noteworthy. The three-aisled interior has a quality of austere grandeur.

The architecture of this group reaches its highest point in the Old Cathedral of Salamanca, begun in 1152 and completed in the first quarter of the thirteenth century (Plate 36). Among the builders was a certain *magister Petri* who worked on the cathedral between 1182 and 1192. The fine and varied decorations of this masterpiece of the Spanish Romanesque are doubtless the joint work of a number of builders and sculptors. Prominent among the carvings are the large sculptures that adorn the springings of the cupola and the many well-designed capitals. These, by a different hand, depict with refinement and a certain idealized naturalism legendary episodes and allegorical and sacred themes. The cupola is similar to that of Zamora and shares its Eastern overtones.

Zamora and Salamanca possess other Romanesque monuments, some containing noteworthy sculpture. The church of La Magdalena in Zamora is particularly worth mentioning. The churches of San Andrés and San Pedro in the same city are built in the same style as the cathedral. The Cathedral of Ciudad Rodrigo, founded by King Ferdinand II about 1165 but not completed until 1230, is the last of the buildings in the group we have just examined. Its porches are decorated with carvings.

In general, art in Asturias remained faithful to the modest tradition of the Ramiran period, but it must be credited with one superlative achievement: the friezes and statuary that adorn the Cámara Santa of Oviedo cathedral, a masterpiece of the Romanesque from the second half of the twelfth century (Plate 39).

In the second half of the twelfth century the plastic arts fell under the influence of certain strongly naturalistic tendencies which rapidly displaced the older styles. During this period the art of the pilgrim route rose to a peak in the sanctuary of Santiago de Compostela, thanks to the emergence of one of the most important sculptors of the European Romanesque, Master Mateo, the first reference to whom occurs in 1161 and the last in 1217. He designed and executed the superb sculpture that adorns the Pórtico de la Gloria in that cathedral (Plate 38). The groups of majestic statues, more lyric than hieratic, clearly reveal the artist's impulse to humanize and the value he placed upon the narrative element. It is clear that from about 1200 Galician sculpture was strongly influenced by the work of this master. The so-called Gelmirez Palace, also in Santiago, is one of the more important achievements of his circle.

Painting

In spite of its remarkable unity, a close examination of Spanish Romanesque painting reveals significant differences that reflect the great stylistic influences of the period—Italian-Byzantine, French, and Mozarabic.

Mural painting was strictly subordinated to the demands of architecture, and no attempt was made to create any kind of illusion. Figures, a very few objects, and decorative arches are molded with austere sensitivity against a plain background, often divided into horizontal bands. The subjects are generally taken from the Bible, the lives of the saints, or allegory, and set off against delicately stylized tracery. Sacred personages are represented in a definite hieratic order, which forms the basis of the frequently symmetrical composition. The Apocalypse and the vision of Ezekiel supply the essential images of this art, which is more suggestive than emotional. The composition, often including inscriptions as well as figures of archangels, seraphim, and apostles.

The style is solemn, majestic, and hieratic, in conformity with the theme, which is almost always presided over by the image of Christ, enthroned, with right hand raised in blessing and an open book in the left. The narrative element is subordinated to the vertical and the static. The firm outlines of the figures accentuate the linearity of the style. The range of gesture and characterization is rather restricted. The artists, who never achieved a final synthesis, are memorable for

their ingenuousness and expressionism. True lighting effects are rare, but there is a great deal of light and shade derived from vigorous modeling.

In the more important paintings the colors used are red, carmine, green, and blue, together with lime white, lampblack, and red and yellow ocher—the more restricted palette of the local painter. The latter strove to extend his chromatic range by mixing his pigments and introducing color contrasts. White was always used for relief and highlights, and black for the outlines of figures and linear detail. Tonal modeling was achieved by means of parallel lines of varying thickness and intensity within each patch of color. As for technique, the mural painters rarely used true fresco, but almost always painted over a light coat of whitewash, which does not absorb the colors like wet lime. Moreover, they often used true fresco for the broad masses of color, filling in the composition in tempera.

Before turning to real Romanesque painting, which owes a great deal to the Mozarabic miniaturists already mentioned, we must draw attention to a number of "archaic" or pre-Romanesque paintings found on the walls of certain Spanish churches. The most important of these are the churches of Tarrasa, San Quirce de Pedret and Marmellá in Catalonia, and Castillejo de Robledo in Castile. The Tarrasa paintings have certain affinities with Roman art of the later period, as illustrated by some of the reliefs in the necropolis at Tarragona, whereas those of San Quirce de Pedret (Plate 34) have more freedom and originality, combining ingenuousness with imagination.

The transition from this archaic quality to the style typical of the Romanesque must have been brought about not so much by natural evolution as by the arrival of artists from centers that still had contacts with Byzantium. Its very nature presupposes a supply of ready-made solutions for all the problems that might have arisen in connection with the thought and taste of an age that was heir to a broad artistic tradition.

To judge from what has been preserved, monumental painting began in Catalonia, where the majority of Spanish Romanesque painting is still to be found. One of the more important artists of the Italian-Byzantine school is the Master of Pedret, not only by virtue of the quality of his work, but also for the relatively large number of paintings attributed to him. His style is a combination of the hieratic tradition of Byzantium and a keen feeling for narrative (Plate 40). He painted the distinctly naturalistic horsemen of the Apocalypse in the apse of San Quirce de Pedret. His grotesque figures in the same church are tremendously alive. He was a great colorist who knew how to heighten the brilliance of his hues by contrasting them with areas of black, thus investing his subjects with dramatic intensity. The historical evidence indicates that the Master of Pedret was chiefly active during the last quarter of the eleventh century. His influence, which extended over a wide area of northern Catalonia, is revealed in the work of a number of lesser painters, with whom his name is associated.

One of the most important groups of Romanesque mural paintings is that from the churches of San Clemente and Santa Maria in the village of Tahull (Lérida). This work reflects the emergence of a strong Italian-Byzantine trend, the date of which can be fixed fairly accurately, thanks to the fact that both churches were consecrated in 1123, apparently to coincide with the completion of the mural decorations.

The Master of San Clemente de Tahull is indeed one of the greatest artists of the European Romanesque, for the originality of his style no less than for the perfection of his technique. Into the central figure of Christ in Glory, between the symbols of the Evangelists, he has introduced minor elements of secondary asymmetry that vary and reinforce the fundamental symmetry of the primary composition. On the curved part of the wall below the vault he has placed, with bold stylization balanced by the architectonic character of the design, the figure of the Virgin and those of various apostles, under a series of decorative arches (Plate 37). It is difficult to know what to admire most in these paintings, the powerful construction or the intense, rich, and vibrant color effects, a basic harmony of red and blue tempered by the white of haloes, robes, arches, and other elements. The ability of the artist is revealed in the strength of characterization that lies behind the hieratic convention.

The apse of Santa Maria de Tahull (Plate 41) was decorated by the Master of Maderuelo, so called for his later work in the Castilian centers of Maderuelo and Berlanga. His talents are similar to those of the Master of San Clemente, but less consistent and vigorous. His

44 (Facing) The Stoning of St.Stephen. Fresco from San Juan de Bohi
(Lérida). Twelfth century. Museum of Ancient Art, Barcelona

45 Master of Maderuelo. The Creation of Man. Detail of a fresco from
Santa Cruz, Maderuelo (Segovia). Twelfth century. The Prado, Madrid

ornamentation, like the stars scattered over the cloak of the Virgin and the details of her throne, is gracefully introduced, without, however, modifying in any way the general architectonic effect. In the church of Vera Cruz de Maderuelo (Segovia), his frescoes covered the vault and walls of the square apsidal chapel (The Prado). In San Baudel de Berlanga (Soria), his series of large Biblical compositions (Museum of Fine Arts, Boston), supplements the work of another painter, the Master of San Baudel, to whom we shall return later.

The decoration of Santa Maria de Tahull can be attributed only partly to the Master of Maderuelo. The rest is the work of another artist with a distinct personality of his own, reflected in an ingenuous but highly expressive style. A lively sense of rhythm and compositional balance might well represent the response of local tradition confronted with a Mediterranean style of Byzantine origin. His sparing color scale, limited to white, black, and red and yellow ocher, pure and in blue-gray, reddish, and yellowish mixtures, tends to confirm this hypothesis. This artist painted an interesting narrative cycle, depicting the Last Judgment and the torments of the damned. Dragons and serpents devour the victims, creating elegant rhythms that recall the early miniaturists. Another fine scene illustrates the end of David's encounter with Goliath (Plate 42).

In the church of San Juan de Bohi, near Tahull, another artist with decided tendencies toward the archaic painted some murals of unusual interest. The figures appear to be lit from the side, a remarkable innovation that shows how the apparent formalism of the Romanesque period was actually based on a genuine taste for experimentation (Plate 44). The painter of the frescoes of the parish church of Sorpe may be presented as typical of the rustic followers of the Master of Tahull. He was a naïve painter but certainly had a gift for narrative painting (Plate 43).

The painter who decorated the central apse of the church of Santa Maria de Mur (Museum of Fine Arts, Boston) is another interesting personality. Though undeniably Byzantine in style, he has affinities with the French school, and, in particular, a preference for setting off figures against a flat light background, rather than against horizontal bands of bright colors (Plate 46). His work is characterized by a dynamic line and airy rhythms. He was willing to distort proportions for the sake of a stronger effect, as in the figure of Christ in Glory. His success in achieving a feeling of space and the freedom of his treatment of the apocalyptic light are equally noteworthy. The paintings that cover the lower part of the curved wall surface reveal his narrative sense, and another side of his talent is evident in the Greek frets and the ornamentation on the windows.

Castile is by no means rich in Romanesque painting, but the little that remains is of high quality. The hermitage of Santa Cruz, in Segovia's hamlet of Maderuelo, was entirely decorated with frescoes, now in the Prado (Plate 45); their author, active in the first half of the twelfth century, is now known as the Master of Maderuelo. His hieratic style displays a close relation to the Italian-Byzantine frescoes. One of the most interesting Castilian monuments is San Baudel de Berlanga (Soria), where the wall paintings covered almost all the interior. Part of the decoration is the work of the Master of Maderuelo, but part is obviously by a different artist (now known as the Master of San Baudel), who either was ignorant of or rejected the Italian-Byzantine formulas. He painted hunting scenes in which the animals are interpreted with sure instinct in a stylized and arbitrary manner and modeled in light tones against a bright red background (Plate 47). There is a strong element Moorish influence in his art, and his style has something in common with certain Hispano-Moresque ivories. In the work of this painter the silhouette assumes a new value, and his compositions are neatly unified by the regularity of rhythms designed to express movement. The frescoes of San Baudel were removed and they are now in the Prado and in the Museum of Fine Arts, in Boston.

We shall conclude our review of monumental Romanesque painting

Overleaf 46, 47 and 48:

(Left) Fresco from the apse of Santa Maria de Mur (Lérida). Twelfth century. Boston Museum of Fine Arts. (Above) Hunting Scene. Fresco from San Baudel de Berlanga (Soria). Twelfth century. The Prado, Madrid. (Below) The Annunciation to the Shepherds. Detail of a fresco in the portico of San Isidoro at León. 1164–1188

with a brief description of a truly magnificent work, unique in Spain for its quality and scope. This is the decoration of the eleventh-century royal funerary chapel of San Isidoro in León, the architecture and sculpture of which we have already had occasion to study. The final touch was applied in the second half of the twelfth century by an unknown painter, with a style that has justly been compared with that of the French miniaturists whose work, dated 1187, is preserved in the same church (Plate 48). These admirable decorations, with their animated and lyrical figures projected against a plain white background, are painted in tempera. They cover the six vaults of the two bays of the portico, together with the east and south walls. The choice of Gospel scenes gave the artist greater freedom in the grouping of his figures, a freedom he exploited with rare inventiveness and imagination, while in some compositions he uses both a preferred ideal plane and a variety of secondary planes derived from the individual rhythms of the vaults. Ornamental friezes of great beauty fill the free spaces and adorn the intervening arches, linking the different compositions in chromatic continuity. The color scale is a rich one, and, though red and yellow ocher, white and black predominate, it also includes blue, green, yellow, and carmine. As for the artist's general style, it is characterized by a tendency to disregard Byzantine conventions and instill life and expression into every scene and detail, which he clearly values for their own sake. At the same time, he never loses sight of the total effect, either of the individual compositions or the decoration as a whole.

49 *St. Martin and the Beggar. Detail of an altar frontal from Montgrony (Gerona). Twelfth century. Archaeological and Artistic Museum, Vich (Barcelona)*

Overleaf 50 and 51:

(Left) Detail of an altar frontal from San Saturnino de Tabérnolas (Lérida). Twelfth century. Museum of Ancient Art, Barcelona. (Right) The Nativity. Detail of an altar frontal from Betesa (Lérida). Thirteenth century. Museum of Ancient Art, Barcelona

97

The Ecclesiastical Workshops

The prevalence of painting on wood panels may have been due to the poverty of the Spanish provinces during the period of the Romanesque. In fact, although we have a few altars made of metal and enamel, like that of San Miguel in Excelsis, or in marble, like that of Tarragona cathedral, such sumptuous pieces are rare. In general, the churches had to be satisfied with liturgical furniture of painted wood. The essential item was an altar table, with decorated front and sides. This was often supplemented with a baldachin, also adorned with ornamental figures and other motifs.

The wooden panel was prepared with a coat of gesso and then painted in tempera, after tracing in the outlines of the design with a punch. The good condition of much of this work, which is particularly abundant in Catalonia, is due both to the thoroughness of the technique and the quality of the pigments. The museums of Barcelona and Vich possess some splendid examples dating from the twelfth and thirteenth centuries.

This church furniture was probably made in workshops attached to the cathedrals and larger monasteries, which, in addition to altars, turned out coffers, carvings, and articles of furniture for ordinary use. The craftsmen often modeled themselves on the great mural painters and miniaturists; at any rate, their subjects are the same: God the Father, Christ in Glory, the Virgin, the apostles, angels, and archangels, scenes from the Testaments and, less frequently, from the lives of the saints. Their art is characterized by the intensity of the colors, among which red and yellow tend to predominate, and by skill in the organization of space by means of firm borders and coherent grouping. The various scenes are neatly separated and often framed with geometrical or floral ornamentation. In almost all cases, the center of the composition is reserved for the figure of Christ or the Virgin, surrounded by a circular or oval aureole. This centerpiece is flanked on either side by narrative scenes or groups of apostles, in hieratical order. In spite of this similarity of theme and style, the tone is brighter than that of the murals, due, no doubt, to the presence of a stronger popular element. Effects achieved by the goldsmiths are imitated, in borders and backgrounds, by means of decorated gesso reliefs.

Several pieces deserve special attention, among them the monumental altar frontal of the bishops, from San Saturnino de Tabérnolas, which is remarkable for the originality of its subject—a simple line of bishops facing the observer—and for the subtlety of its restrained color scale of sienna and chestnut-brown ochers (Plate 50). In the altar frontals from Ix and the Cathedral of Urgel, on the other hand, the color combinations are almost violent. Another altar, devoted to St. Martin, made in the workshops of Ripoll, reveals a fine sense of narrative (Plate 49). The examples with the representation of the Virgin and St. Margaret, from the workshops of Vich, were painted in the twelfth century, like all the pieces we have mentioned so far (Plate 52). The Neo-Byzantine style of the first half of the thirteenth century is evident in the altar frontals of Valltarga, Orellá, and Betesa (Plate 51). All these examples are from Catalonia, since work of this kind is seldom found in Aragon and Castile.

Between the eleventh and thirteenth century the ecclesiastical sculptors also devoted their talents to carving church furniture, retables, and ivories. Most of the time they worked in wood. Once a piece had been carved, it was coated with gesso and painted in polychromy with great decorative skill. As a result, it is often difficult to separate this sort of carving from monumental sculpture. During this period forms were simple, very expressive, but almost always rigid. The passage of time brought an increasing interest in the representation of movement and a greater taste for lyricism, which was superimposed on the hieratic conventions of the Romanesque.

The basic themes are Christ on the Cross and Mary, the Virgin Mother, subjects endlessly repeated, with variations depending on the spirit of the school and the inspiration of the artist. Saints and Biblical figures are also represented, the elaborate compositions depicting the Descent from the Cross being of particular interest.

The ivories deserve our attention both for the nobility of the material and for the antiquity of the pieces. A good deal of eleventh-century work has been preserved, in the form of crosses, caskets, crosiers, bookbindings, pyxes, and so forth. The ivories of the Spanish Romanesque often betray the influence of the Moorish carvers of Cordova and Cuenca. At the same time, they bear a definite resemblance to certain Northern work, specifically that of the German ivory

52 *The Flagellation of St. Margaret. Detail of an altar frontal from Vich (Barcelona). Twelfth century. Archaeological and Artistic Museum, Vich (Barcleona)*

53 (Left) Cross donated to San Isidoro at León by Ferdinand I and Sancha. 1063. Ivory

54 (Right) Christ of Mitgarán (Lérida). Twelfth century. Polychrome wood

carvers of the Rhine valley. One of the outstanding pieces of the period is the cross of San Isidoro in León, donated by Ferdinand I and Sancha in 1063 (Plate 53). The simplicity of the modeling of the naked body of Christ makes a strong contrast with the elaborate workmanship of the cross, which is edged with tiny figures, treated as ornament.

In wooden sculpture Catalonia possesses several fine versions of Christ in Majesty, with the ample tunics (Plate 57) that define the type, as well as the Christ of Mitgarán, a fragment of a Descent from the Cross, remarkable for its quality and its blend of primitiveness and expressionism (Plate 54). The best figures of the Virgin Mary are in the cathedrals of Gerona and Solsona, and in the monastery of Montserrat. The Museum of Catalan Art and the museums of Marés and Vich, among others, possess many magnificent sculptures of this type, carved with sobriety, elegance, and a sense of the hieratic. Altar frontals, carved in relief and finished in polychromy, like those of San Pedro de Ripoll and Tahull, are comparable to the work of the monumental painters in beauty and strength.

There is an unusual abundance of later work, that is to say, work from the second half of the thirteenth century, a period during which monumental sculpture was already advancing with confident steps along the pathways of the Gothic style.

The Minor Arts

Spain is fortunate in still possessing an excellent and representative collection of work in the various minor arts of the Romanesque period. At that time the distinction between the fine and the applied arts was not as rigid as, for sociological as well as artistic reasons, it was later to become. The medieval craftsman might well be, and in fact often was, an unusually gifted artist. Apart from its considerable aesthetic value, his work is of human and historical interest in that it throws light on various aspects of the life and culture of the eleventh, twelfth, and thirteenth centuries. Though his tools and materials were simple and few, the skill and sensitivity with which he handled them are often truly astonishing. The goldsmith's work, embroideries, enamels, and furniture of the Spanish Romanesque yield nothing to painting and sculpture in the strength and purity of their style. Nor must we forget the great illuminated books, precious indeed for the devoted labor that went into their making and for the beauty of the ornamentation.

The greatest among the many achievements of the Spanish metalworkers of the Romanesque is the silver altar of the Cámara Santa in the cathedral of Oviedo. This piece, with Biblical figures of great finesse worked in *repoussé*, dates from about 1075. Other outstanding examples of the art include the cross of Mansilla de la Sierra, the Loarre coffer in engraved copper, the diptych of Oviedo, and several chalices, the finest of which is that given to San Isidoro in León by the Infanta Doña Urraca during the last quarter of the eleventh century. Simplicity of form, emphasis on architectonic and plastic values, and intense ornamentation are the more important characteristics of this work. To these we should add, at least in relation to some of the pieces, a taste for precious and semiprecious stones, derived from the barbaric and late Roman styles.

The furniture-maker is well represented by the chair of Roda, with elaborate carvings of the same fabulous animals that decorate the initial letters in illuminated manuscripts, the so-called chest of the Cid, and the polychrome coffer of Astorga. During the thirteenth century Romanesque furniture acquired certain Mudejar characteristics, which it was to retain all through the Gothic period and even beyond.

As for embroidery, Catalonia possesses a twelfth-century tapestry of really extraordinary quality, by European as well as by Spanish standards: this is the huge and splendid tapestry of the Creation in the Cathedral of Gerona (Plate 58). The name is derived from the subject: the figure of the Savior surrounded by allegorical subjects and personifications of the winds, the seasons, the months, and the days of the Creation, all organized in an essentially circular and radial composition. The figures of men and animals are depicted with delicacy and ingenuous grace. The style is more closely related to that of the miniature than to monumental painting. Other interesting embroideries include the banner of San Ot, and an altar frontal from the Cathedral of Urgel, now in the Victoria and Albert Museum, London.

A number of unique pieces of twelfth- and thirteenth-century Romanesque enamelwork are still preserved in their places of origin. Among them are the shrine of Santo Domingo de Silos in Burgos (Plate 55), the altar frontal of the church of San Miguel in Excelsis in Navarre, the crucifix of the Cathedral of Urgel, and the Virgin of La Vega in Salamanca cathedral. They are distinguished by a remarkable synthesis of color, *repoussé* work, metallic luster, and stylistic expression. The color scale is primarily blue, green, and yellow, with occasional touches of red and white. Harmonizing with the bronze and gilded silver, these hues produce effects of incomparable richness. Crosses, reliquaries, caskets, pyxes, crosiers, sword hilts, and other objects made of silver or enameled bronze have been preserved in relatively large numbers.

As we have seen, the Mozarabs were particularly successful as miniaturists, assimilating various Eastern influences and paving the way for the Romanesque. Through the centuries that followed, numerous specially trained monks, working in the scriptoria attached to monasteries and cathedrals, were employed in painstakingly copying manuscripts, decorating the parchment with intricately illuminated letters and stylized scenes. Of course, Carolingian and Ottonian in-

55 Shrine from Santo Domingo de Silos (Burgos). Champlevé enamel on copper. Twelfth century. Archaeological Museum, Burgos

56 (Facing) Page from the Prayer Book of Doña Sancha. Signed by Fructuoso in 1055. University of Santiago de Compostela (Coruña)

fluences, with their Byzantine overtones, continued to work upon the Mozarabic base. The earliest manuscripts with unmistakably Romanesque illumination appeared during the eleventh century. They are written in Visigothic characters; the Carolingian uncial script was not adopted in Castile until the beginning of the twelfth century, though it had been in use in Catalonia since the tenth, doubtless because of the direct cultural influence exerted by Carolingian France on the territory of the Spanish March.

Within its more modest limits, Romanesque illumination has the same qualities of monumentality and nobility of form and the same sense of structure as the monumental paintings of the period. The drawing is just as vigorous and the stylization equally true and expressive. Much of this work, without departing from Romanesque formulas, has a distinctly popular flavor, quite different from the courtliness of the French Romanesque. On the other hand, there is no difference in atmosphere, in the treatment of space, or in the relation of the figures to each other and to the superficial elements representing

106

objects. The poses and gestures are well diversified and, though rigid, retain an air of gracefulness, even when they might be thought a trifle forced. Arabesques, spirals, and parallel lines in different tones were used to model form, at the same time imparting a feeling of ornamentality, which the artist ingeniously echoed in the linear rhythms of his figures and decorative motifs.

One of the finest illuminated books of the Spanish Romanesque is

57 (Facing) Christ. Twelfth century. Polychrome wood. Museum of Ancient Art, Barcelona

58 Embroidered Tapestry of the Creation. Twelfth century. Cathedral of Gerona

a montes qui
in esebon · & og
qui mansit in a
edrai transiordi
moab · coepitq;
explanare leg
D nr dñi loquit
horeb dic: Sui
in hoc monte m
uer timini & in
monte amorr
cetera quae eis
campestria atq;
na · & humilior
tra meridie & iu
maris · terra cl
& lybani · usq; c
magnu eufrati
quit tradidi uo
mini · & possde
qua iurauit dñ
uris abraham
cob · ut daret ille
meous post eos
Dixiq; uob illo
solus sustinere

INRPT LIBER

the Beatus of the Cathedral of Burgo de Osma of 1086, with miniatures signed by Martin. Books of this type, a legacy of Mozarabic times, provided the illuminators of the period with a series of fascinating motifs in which they were to specialize for two centuries. No less important than the Beatus of Burgo de Osma are the prayer book of Ferdinand I and Doña Sancha of 1055 (Plate 56), signed by Fructuoso (University of Santiago de Compostela), and the *Book of the Testaments* (Oviedo cathedral) of the first third of the twelfth century. In the latter the artist's exceptional powers are revealed in fourteen miniatures, illustrating acts of donation, and in the beauty of his ornamental calligraphy. The exquisite designs are gorgeously clothed in colors of gold, silver, red, green, and purple.

From Aragon comes the Bible of Huesca (National Archaeological Museum, Madrid). In its illuminations we can see a parallel to the carved capitals of the period, floral motifs mingling with linear elements that may turn with equal ease into the simple outlines of a letter of the alphabet or the body, neck, and head of a real or fabulous animal. In the thirteenth century, Aragonese miniatures were distinctly Byzantine in character, like the mural decorations of Sijena.

Many of the best of these illuminations are doubtless the work of native miniaturists; at the same time, in view of the roving life led by the medieval craftsmen, some may be by artists from across the Pyrenees. The most important Catalonian scriptoria were at Ripoll, Vich, and Cuxa. The first of these was responsible for the Bible of Ripoll (Vatican Library), and the Bible of Roda, now in the Bibliothèque Nationale, Paris (Plate 59), both from the eleventh century and both containing large numbers of miniatures in delicate tints.

59 Page from the Bible of Roda (Gerona). Eleventh century. Bibliothèque Nationale, Paris

Chapter IV

The Late Middle Ages

GOTHIC ARCHITECTURE

The early Gothic architecture of Spain is often described as "transitional." The term is not inappropriate if applied to the buildings rather than the style, for this so-called transition is more a juxtaposition of different structural principles than an evolving architectural concept. The first element of the Gothic to be introduced into Spain was the ribbed vault. This was followed by the abandonment of semicircular chapels in favor of a polygonal plan. Many "transitional" buildings have mixed vaulting. Buildings designed exclusively in the new style did not appear until the early part of the thirteenth century.

The gradual acceptance of the Gothic style was due, in no small measure, to the influence of the Cistercians. In their love of simplicity and bare monumentality, Cistercian architects frequently chose as their model the plainest and least ornamented of the twelfth-century churches built by their order. Moreruela, founded in 1131, was the first Cistercian monastery on Spanish soil. In 1162 the monastery of Santa Maria de la Huerta was built on the frontier between Castile and Aragon, while at the end of the century the monastery of Santa Maria de Valbuena was founded on the banks of the Douro. In Catalonia there arose the great monasteries of Poblet and Santas Creus. The church of the former, which, with its length of more than three hundred feet, might well rival a cathedral, is one of the finest examples of the severity of the style. Founded sometime after 1166, it must have been completed in the final years of the same century. Like other Cistercian monasteries, Poblet is architecturally interesting not only for its church but also for its secondary structures: cloister, chapter house, dormitories, libraries, walled enclosures, and monumental gates. The church of Santas Creus, more typically Cistercian, has a large square apse, flanked on either side by two square apsidal chapels set in either arm of a transept, and three aisles separated by cruciform columns. Though probably begun in 1174, it was not completed until some fifty years later. The churches of Fitero, Veruela, Sacramenia, and Córcoles are also Cistercian. All contain elements characteristic of early Spanish Gothic, which was to culminate in the powerful and original Cathedral of Avila. In this cathedral, which incorporates work of various periods, the foremost influence is Burgundian. The structure is unusual in providing an early example of the use of a six-partite vault.

The thirteenth century saw the consolidation of the material progress made in the twelfth. The victory at Las Navas de Tolosa (1212) gave a powerful new impetus to the reconquest. The reign of Ferdinand III (1217–1252) witnessed a series of important political events, including the unification of Castile and León in 1230. Relations with France were very close. Priests, pilgrims, artists, and soldiers poured into Spain from the surrounding countries, some drawn by the pilgrimage route to Santiago de Compostela or the struggle against Islam, others in the wake of the alliances contracted by the royal family. All this helped to spread and popularize the Gothic style. Of course, numerous churches continued to be built or planned along archaic or Romanesque lines.

The first wholly Gothic structure to be built in Spain was probably the church of the Hospice of Roncesvalles, begun about 1209. Modeled on the churches of northern France, it may well be the work of a French architect. The next stage in the advance of the Gothic style is marked by the Cathedral of Cuenca. Its architect, trained in Soissons and Laon, completed the six-partite vaults of the east end in about 1225. Another interesting early Gothic cathedral is that of Sigüenza, with an imposing façade framed by two immense square towers that give it a fortress-like appearance.

As the thirteenth century progressed, the cities continued to acquire political and economic power at the expense of the countryside, and great cathedrals began to arise.

The cornerstone of Toledo cathedral was laid in 1226, under Ferdinand III. The great cathedral, which measures almost four hundred feet in length and two hundred feet in width, was begun by one Master Martin, but is mostly the work of Petrus Petri, who died in 1291. The cathedral has five aisles, and large transepts, with the main chapel enclosed by a double ambulatory. The result is an original concept of space, in which the vertical thrust is much more restrained than in most of the buildings directly inspired by French or Northern influence.

In its present form, the Toledo cathedral is perhaps the most representative of all the cathedrals of Spain. Its picturesque superposition of styles is the result of five centuries of unceasing architectural activity, during which a succession of memorial chapels, mostly the gift of nobles and princes, has been added to the original Gothic structures. Here, both inside and out, the unifying principle is the

60 (Left) Cathedral of Burgos. Thirteenth century

61 (Right) Cathedral of León. Thirteenth century

spirit rather than the form. Fortress-like and weathered to a golden brown—so different from the gray of the French cathedrals—by the hot sun of Castile, Toledo is a symbol of the Spanish sense of religious worship. At the same time, it constitutes a synthesis of the diverse elements in Spanish art, like the cusped arches of the gallery above the ambulatory, Plateresque construction, and work in the purest Renaissance style. This, however, strengthens rather than undermines the unity of the structure, adding a historical factor, that is also observable in other Spanish cathedrals. In fact, it is precisely this sort of vigorous assimilation that gives Spanish architecture its unique character. In the course of time, Toledo cathedral has been endowed with numerous works of art that have turned it into one of the great museums of Spain.

Another important Gothic cathedral is that of Burgos, begun in 1222 and consecrated in 1260, on completion of the transept. The spired towers and the lantern over the crossing were completed during the fifteenth and early sixteenth centuries (Plate 60). Burgos differs from Toledo not only in its closer adherence to French models, but also in its freedom from Mudejar elements. It is a building conceived in the Northern spirit and erected at the meeting point of two races and two civilizations. The impressiveness of its elegant structure is enhanced by the superior quality of its unusually abundant sculpture, which covers the porches and towers and even extends to the interior arcades. The cathedral was given its crowning touch with the addition of the Constable's Chapel, a gem of Plateresque art.

The Cathedral of León is especially interesting, not only for the purity of its style, related to Reims and Chartres, but also because, unlike Burgos, the Gothic fabric has remained untouched and free of later additions and modifications (Plate 61). Its construction must have cost a tremendous effort, since León was not a wealthy diocese, particularly after it ceased to be the seat of the royal court. Only the determination of the prelate, Don Martin Fernández, appointed in 1254, carried the project forward. The highest parts of the structure were not added until the fifteenth century. The richly carved west front contains three great doors, beneath a gable wall with rose windows, niches, and arcades. Designed as a Latin cross with very short arms, the interior of the cathedral, with its long chancel and chevet of five six-sided chapels, reflects the same purity of style as its exterior. The many stained-glass windows and the height of the narrow nave contribute much to the general impression of airiness and light.

During the thirteenth century, cathedrals, churches, and monasteries were also built in the central and western parts of Spain. The cathedral of Cuenca and Burgo de Osma should be mentioned for the originality of their lighting and quality of decoration. The cathedral of Tuy was practically completed by Bishop Esteban Egea (1218–1239). There is a fine carved door in the gabled west wall.

The greatest of the monasteries is that of Las Huelgas at Burgos. The church, chapter house, and cloister, all built in the same style, belong to the reign of Ferdinand III. The French influence here is very strong, and the architecture has obvious affinities with that of Anjou.

The fourteenth century was a period of assimilation and slow development rather than stylistic innovation, and its aspect varied from one region to the next. In central and western Spain construction continued on the great churches begun during the course of the previous century. Here we find some infiltration of Mudejar influence, based on Nasrid art. Castile and León, now united, were the scene of civil wars between royalist and usurping factions, as in the struggle between Pedro I and Henry II (Trastamara). These often led to foreign intervention, and there were numerous economic crises.

Among the churches built in the center and west of Spain during this period, we must not fail to mention the Cathedral of Lugo, the chancel of which was begun shortly after 1308, and that of Palencia, its cornerstone laid in 1321. Both buildings reflect the influence of the Cathedral of Burgos and the progress of construction was very slow.

In 1373, Vitoria, the Basque capital, was taken from Navarre by Castile. Shortly before this, work had begun on its cathedral. The Basque churches of the Gothic period did not transform the style, but neutralized it, partly by emphasizing the robust popular vein. Many were modeled on the Cathedral of León and, though rustic and simple, are very picturesque. For example, in Castro Urdiales, the church of Santa Maria rises above a small promontory that juts out into the sea. Part of a small cluster of medieval structures, including a boldly arched bridge, it has the air of a brave little fortress.

Toward the end of the century, two important churches were built

62 *(Left) Interior of the Cathedral of Seville. Fifteenth century*

63 *(Right) Interior of "La Lonja" of Palma (Majorca). Fifteenth century*

near Toledo by a Master Alfonso, who had previously worked on the great cathedral of that city. These are the chapel of the Jeronymite convent of Guadalupe and the collegiate church of Talavera de la Reina. Both structures have numerous Mudejar elements.

The Kingdom of Catalonia and Aragon enjoyed increasing prosperity, the beginnings of which can be traced to the conquest of Majorca and Valencia and the period of Mediterranean expansion in the thirteenth century. Building activity was at a high level and included much civil as well as religious construction. The architecture is distinguished by its austerity and severely restrained decoration, giving rise to a very characteristic form of Gothic that has been labeled "functional" and which represents less the influence of Provence and

Languedoc than the evolution of architectural thinking in Catalonia itself.

Begun with apses in the Romanesque style, and completed, with a west front in the Gothic manner, Tarragona Cathedral is a fine example of medieval Catalan architecture. It differs from the French, as well as from the Castilian, in its greater simplicity and "functionalism." Moreover, the horizontal articulation is no less important than the vertical, vigorous buttresses that punctuate the heavy walls. This concept was developed during the fourteenth century, at the very height of the Gothic period, as may be seen, for example, in Barcelona. During that century Barcelona gained pre-eminence over the other cities of Catalonia, as reflected in its monuments.

Among its one-aisled churches the finest are the elegant chapel of Santa Agueda, adjoining the royal palace and begun by Bertran de Riquer in 1302, the parish church of Santa Maria del Pino, with an exterior strongly characterized by heavy prismatic masses, and the convent of Pedralbes, founded in 1326. Sometimes the plan is further modified to include chapels between the chancel buttresses as well as between those of the nave. Churches of this type are particularly common in Palma de Majorca, where San Francisco, San Jaime, and La Santa Cruz are representative.

Although in some ways related to the cathedrals of Toulouse and Narbonne, Barcelona cathedral is essentially an original design. Construction began in 1298 and continued intermittently until the towers were completed almost a century later. The exterior of the cathedral has several interesting features, including the strict geometry of the chancel walls and the severe Door of San Ivo, which is on the north side. The three-aisled interior creates an impression of mystical grandeur. The narrowness of the interior is emphasized by the wide spacing of the columns, the low capitals of which are carved with naturalistic floral motifs. The cathedral has a number of unusual structural characteristics: the placing of the lantern over the last bay of the center aisle, the construction of belfries above the outside bays of the arms of the transept, and the broad galleries running above the chapels and opening onto the side aisles.

Barcelona has another important fourteenth-century church in Santa Maria del Mar. Begun in 1328 under the direction of Berenguer de Montagut, its architecture is an expression of austerity and grandeur.

The Cathedral of Gerona was begun by Master Enrique, who was succeeded by Jacobo de Favarán, builder of the Cathedral of Narbonne. Work on the single, majestic aisle, with a clear span of more than seventy-five feet, continued well into the fourteenth century. The exterior of the cathedral is a good example of the general tendency of Catalan Gothic toward functional simplicity, its six huge buttresses projecting starkly beyond bare stone walls.

The structural types we have just examined are to be found scattered all over the Kingdom of Catalonia and Aragon. Some of the larger buildings took three or four centuries to complete. Such was the case with the imposing Cathedral of Majorca, almost 400 feet long and 180 feet wide, which was begun sometime before 1323.

Throughout the century, convents and churches for the mendicant orders continued to be built. Galician examples of this group include the church of the monastery of Santo Domingo de Bonaval, in Santiago de Compostela, which has three aisles, a transept, and three apses, San Francisco de Lugo, and San Francisco de Orense.

In the Kingdom of Catalonia and Aragon the improvement in social and economic conditions was reflected in the construction of a number of fine buildings of a civil type. The royal palace of Barcelona, adjoining the cathedral, was enlarged by the addition of the great hall "del Tinell," begun in 1359 by Master Guillermo Carbonell. Its huge semicircular arches rest on columns set against the walls. Other important civil buildings in Barcelona include the Town Hall, with its splendid façade built sometime after 1399 by Arnau Bargues, and the "Lonja," or exchange, close by the sea. To these we should add the shipyard complex, where galleys were constructed and repaired. This had been in existence since the first half of the thirteenth century, but was rebuilt by Pedro the Ceremonious after 1378 and enlarged again during the fifteenth century.

Much of the military construction of the fourteenth century is also of interest. The castle of Bellver in Majorca, circular in plan, has a courtyard with a double gallery. The monastery of Poblet was dignified by the addition of the beautiful Royal Gate. This was the model for the even more monumental Gate of "Serranos" in Valencia, completed in 1398. Other fourteenth-century military construction of considerable architectural interest is to be found in the interior of Spain. All these castles, with their rugged silhouettes and walls burned golden by the sun, are one of the striking features of the Castilian countryside. Many are well-preserved and impressively carved and decorated. The building of cathedrals continued into the fifteenth century; those at Oviedo and Pamplona are the most interesting.

There can be no doubt, however, that the greatest achievement of fifteenth-century Spanish architecture is the Cathedral of Seville, not only because of its extraordinary size, 475 feet long and 250 feet wide, but also because it represents a synthesis of the different elements of the Spanish style. There are five aisles, the one in the center rising to a height of more than 118 feet; this induces a feeling of the infinite, which an Islamic builder would have achieved by other means. The vaults are all cross vaults, except for those redesigned as star vaults by Gil de Hontañón early in the sixteenth century. The decoration rises to a climax in the center bay of the crossing, where above each of the side arches three windows pierce the wall at a height of 138 feet (Plate 62). The east end of the cathedral shows signs of the approach of the Renaissance, with rectangular chapels on either side of the projecting choir. In a return to ancient custom, made necessary by the location of the cathedral, the main doors, including the beautifully carved Door of the Nativity, open into the east end of the church. As in all such cases, the Cathedral of Seville was destined to exert its influence over an enormous area. The architects of a number of Andalusian churches built around the year 1500 clearly used it as a model.

During the fifteenth century, a great deal of time was also spent in completing and decorating churches begun in the course of the two centuries that had preceded it, particularly in finishing the loftier parts of the structure: lanterns, vaulting, towers and steeples, pinnacles and cresting, and in adding cloisters, sacristies, and sumptuous memorial chapels for prelates and grandees. Thus, the great tower of Toledo cathedral was erected between 1424 and 1452, and the spires of Burgos cathedral between 1442 and 1458, under the direction of the German master, Johan of Cologne, while in 1472 the cloister of Segovia cathedral was begun by Juan Guas. Inside these buildings, the geometry of the vaulting becomes increasingly complex, whether it be purely

64   Castle of Olite (Navarre). Fourteenth century

Gothic, as in the churches of Burgos, or essentially Mudejar, as in Saragossa cathedral.

In the history of Gothic architecture and sculpture the beautiful memorial chapels are a chapter in themselves. Their prototype is that built in Toledo cathedral for Cardinal Gil de Albornoz in the middle of the fifteenth century. Prominent among these fifteenth-century chapels are the chapel of Don Alvaro de Luna, master of Santiago, which is in Toledo cathedral, and that of Don Pedro Fernández de Velasco, the constable of Castile, in Burgos cathedral. The first of these was begun in 1432, but in 1448 the work was entrusted to Hanequin of Brussels, who is doubtless responsible for its flowery qualities. The second, of later date, was built about 1500 by Simon, son of Johan of Cologne. Its walls are adorned with a series of great

123

escutcheons with bearers, and the cornices and moldings are exquisitely carved. Many such memorial chapels embellish the cathedrals, churches, and monasteries of Spain.

During the first seventy-five years of the fifteenth century, as in the latter part of the fourteenth, the finest civil buildings were those erected in Catalonia and the east. The close political and economic ties with France and Italy made it necessary to build numbers of palaces, exchanges, and halls. In 1416 the Deputies of Catalonia decided to restore an existing building, entrusting the work to Marcos Safont. The façade was embellished with carvings by Pedro Johan, while part of the interior was converted into a fine patio surrounded by a gallery with slender pointed arches.

The "Lonja" of Palma, built by Master Guillermo Sagrera between 1426 and 1451, is nobly proportioned, its bare, battlemented walls, flanked with slender octagonal towers, contrasting strongly with the wealth of sober ornamentation around the doors and windows. The interior, a great hall 120 feet long and 80 feet wide, is divided into four bays covered with cross vaults supported on spiral-fluted piers (Plate 63). Sagrera also built the great hall of the Castel Nuovo in Naples, for Alfonso V of Aragon. At this time the influence of Catalan architecture was felt in Roussillon, Sardinia, Naples, and Sicily, and even in Cyprus and Rhodes.

The outstanding secular structure in the northern part of Spain is the magnificent castle of Olite, built by order of Charles III (Charles the Noble) of Navarre (1387–1425). Unfortunately, the richly decorated interior, mostly in the Mudejar style, has been destroyed by fire and war (Plate 64).

THE ISABELLA OF CASTILE STYLE

The last phase of fifteenth-century Gothic, during which Flemish and German influences mingled with a tradition nourished by the art of Moslem Spain, is known as the "Isabella of Castile style." Chronologically, it coincides with the reign of Queen Isabella of Castile (1474–1504), giving way, during the first quarter of the sixteenth century, to the Plateresque style, although certain Gothic forms lingered on, modified in varying degrees by the taste of the Renaissance.

124

In decoration the Isabella of Castile style makes use of the flamboyant and more florid elements of the Gothic, but limits them to well-defined areas, in the Moorish manner. On the other hand, there appears to have been a preference for carving in wood rather than in stone. The façades are influenced by the great retables, and a profusion of ornament conceals structures that are really quite simple. Certain decorative motifs, like escutcheons and heraldic animals, are given particular prominence, and objects like the trunks and roots of trees are represented in a naturalistic way. Sculpture is placed against intricate backgrounds, laboriously carved with all-over patterns of shells, fish, balls, clubs, or basketwork. This art could hardly have developed so rapidly without the passion for building that possessed the Catholic Kings, still less without the presence and prestige of a number of outstanding artists, equally talented as architects and sculptors. These were Hanequin of Brussels, whose work in Toledo cathedral had started a school; Juan Guas, son of a Frenchman, Pedro, and possibly the central figure of the group; Simon de Colonia, son of a German; and Gil de Siloé, best known for his sculpture.

One of the first monuments in the Isabella of Castile style is the church of the Carthusian monastery of Miraflores, near Burgos. The greater part of the monastery was built in 1461, but the church was added later. The work was begun by Garcia Fernández de Matienzo and continued, after 1478, by Simon de Colonia. Inside, the beautiful choir is roofed with star vaults and profusely decorated.

One of the finest achievements of the Isabella of Castile period is the church of San Juan de los Reyes in Toledo, built by Juan Guas in 1476. Remarkable for its perfect unity of style, the interior is decorated with great friezes of escutcheons, supported by eagles, and Gothic inscriptions obviously inspired by the calligraphic ornamentation of the Moors. A similar influence is observable in the treatment of the ribs of the transept vaults, the arches of the gallery over the cloister, and other areas of carving.

The ornamental aspects of the Isabella of Castile style are most strikingly expressed in the façades of two buildings in Valladolid, the church of the monastery of San Pablo and the Colegio di San Gregorio. The façade of San Pablo, with its groups of reliefs superimposed on an intricately worked and subdivided background, was built between 1485

65   Alcázar of Segovia. Fifteenth century

66   (Facing) Detail of a portal, Colegio di San Gregorio, Valladolid. Fifteenth century

and 1499. In the contemporary façade of the Colegio di San Gregorio the architectural composition is literally buried beneath the ornamentation, centered upon a huge royal coat of arms (Plate 66). The Colegio has a magnificent interior court surrounded by a lofty gallery with decoration almost as elaborate as that of the façade.

During the last quarter of the fifteenth century, the kings and the nobility developed a taste for imposing and lavishly decorated palaces. The simple façades of the earlier part of the century gave way to designs, more ostentatious and heavily ornamental, that better reflected the architectural preferences of the times. Typical of these palaces are the Alcázar of Segovia (Plate 65) and the magnificent Infantado ducal palace in Guadalajara, with its splendid façade and profusely decorated patio, the work of Juan Guas and other masters.

GOTHIC SCULPTURE

The Gothic sculpture of Spain, at first a mere continuation of the late Romanesque, soon fell under the direct influence of artists arriving from France. Monumental and decorative sculpture was carved in stone, marble, and alabaster, and often painted. Architectural carving was designed to fit neatly into the structure, especially around doorways, where statues were set against the jambs, and where reliefs were used freely. The monumental tombs, with the recumbent effigies of the dead and the reliefs depicting the funeral or the ascent of the soul to heaven, are often the finest ornament of the chapels that contain them. As for the altar, its essential decorative element was the retable, and though most of these were painted, some were beautifully carved, especially during the later stages of the Gothic. The subjects are taken from the Gospels and concentrated around the figure of Christ, often

67 (Left) Christ. Tympa-
num of the Sarmental Door,
Cathedral of Burgos. c. 1230

68 (Right) Alfonso X and
Doña Violante. Figures in
the cloister of the Cathedral
of Burgos. Thirteenth century. Stone

enthroned. The twelve apostles, the Evangelists, angels, and archangels
are other themes that constantly recur in portals and retables. Scenes
from the lives of the saints, alternating with Biblical allusions, gave the
Gothic genius for narrative an ample opportunity to unfold.

During the three centuries of its existence, the style gradually lost
its initial rigidity, inherited from the Romanesque. An idealized
naturalism, prompted by the religious feeling of the age as much as by
aesthetic considerations, prevents a tendency to do justice to the model
from degenerating into vulgar realism. The effect is further enhanced
by a refined elegance, partly derived from the drapery and gestures of
the period. To some extent the character of the sculpture is determined by the subordination of groups of figures to the geometry of
the architecture. The polychromy does not entirely offset this, since it,
too, is far from being merely imitative.

During the last quarter of the fourteenth century, under the in-

69 *(Left) The White Virgin. Detail. Main door, Cathedral of León. Thirteenth century*

70 *(Right) The Last Judgment. Tympanum of the main door, Cathedral of León. Thirteenth century*

fluence of the Franco-Burgundian school and, in particular, of Claus Sluter, Gothic naturalism became more pronounced. The style grew broader, richer, and somewhat more rhetorical. Draperies lost some of their original simplicity and began to fall in tight, rhythmic folds.

During the fifteenth century the plastic arts were in an unsettled state, and by the second half of the century Northern and Mudejar ornamentalism was beginning to undermine the purity of the naturalistic style. Nevertheless, we have some excellent examples of its formal austerity, touched now by the spirit of the Renaissance, among them the tomb of Martín Vázquez de Arce in Sigüenza.

The subtle stylization and avoidance of strict frontality that define Gothic art are also apparent in some of the sculpture of the late Romanesque, for example, the carvings by Master Mateo in the Pórtico de la Gloria in the Cathedral of Santiago de Compostela.

At the beginning of the second quarter of the thirteenth century, though unconnected with the above, there appeared the abundant sculpture of Burgos cathedral, highly varied within the terms of its unity of style and wholly Gothic. Some of this work dates from the first phase of construction, about 1230, some from the beginning of the second, around 1240, while a third group corresponds to another period of activity twenty years later. The carvings, doubtless the most ancient, that adorn the Sarmental Door in the south façade of the transept, are the work of two artists from Amiens. Their style is characterized by noble proportions, a classical clarity of form, and the clever organization of space. Lines and flourishes that might have ornamental value are kept to a minimum, while the masses are brought out forcefully, but without disturbing the serenity of the whole.

The Coronería Door in the north wall of the transept is probably the work of Master Enrique (died 1277), architect, sculptor, designer, master builder of the Cathedral of León. The style is more Spanish than that of the sculpture around the Sarmental Door, that is to say, a shade less refined but more powerfully expressive (Plate 67). The upper parts of the exterior are also decorated with sculpture of exceptional quality, carved about 1260. Here the idealistic naturalism of the Gothic is more pronounced than in the work we have reviewed so far. The courtly spirit is now allied with religious feeling and a strange lyricism of form, which is handled with increasing freedom, as revealed in the gestures, the folds of the loose cloaks, and other details. The numerous heads that decorate the triforium inside the cathedral must have come from the same workshop.

More interesting carvings are to be found in the cloister, reached through a door which itself is handsomely carved. The columns and galleries of the cloister are adorned with groups of statues that illustrate the diversity of the Gothic sculpture of the period. The group representing Alfonso X and his wife, Doña Violante, is especially noteworthy (Plate 68). In these figures the idea of a portrait has been fully realized without detracting from the strictly plastic values.

In the Cathedral of León, the range of sculpture, from the second half of the thirteenth century, is even broader than at Burgos. The three doors of the west front with its portico, the transept doors, and the interior with its beautiful funerary monuments represent a cross section of the plastic arts of the early Gothic. Clearly there were three principal sculptors, whose personalities are distinctly expressed. The foremost of the three, to whom the more important groups were entrusted, is none other than the man who carved the statues for the Coronería Door in Burgos cathedral. His stone image of the Virgin and Child, known as the White Virgin, is one of the finest sculptures ever made in Spain (Plate 69). The noble severity of his style stands opposed to the greater freedom and imagination of the second of the three sculptors of León, known only as the Master of the Last Judgment, whose narrative poetry is very personal and profoundly Spanish (Plate 70). The third master carved the apostles on the jambs of the south door and many statues in the main façade. The style of this artist is more restrained, closer to the manner of the French masters from Amiens who carved the Sarmental Door at Burgos.

During the thirteenth century, the introduction of the Gothic style by artists from the north of France was paralleled by an independent evolution toward the new forms. This was characterized by lingering traces of the Romanesque, particularly a certain archaism and a taste for the ornamental interpretation of structure and detail. One of the best demonstrations of the potentialities of this art is the tomb of the Infante Don Felipe (died 1274) and his wife, Leonor Rodríguez de Castro, in Villalcázar de Sirga (Plate 71). The faces of the tomb are carved with scenes of mourning, set between bands of heraldic ornament. The two recumbent figures, both of great beauty, reveal the sculptor's interest in the details of dress, though at no time does he lose sight of the general design. This work is attributed to the sculptor Antón Pérez de Carrión and is remarkable for its freshness and originality.

Gothic sculpture had a very important role to play, both in architecture and directly as imagery. The influence of the great stone-cutting centers and workshops was gradually to transform the face of Spanish style. In most churches the doors were decorated with sculpture and, inside, the tombs and chapel walls were richly carved and embellished with reliefs and statues. Crucifixions, Descents from the Cross, enthroned effigies of the Virgin, and statues of saints, prophets, monarchs, and prelates introduced a human note into religious architecture. Burgos, León, Zamora, Salamanca, Soria, and Avila have

71 *Tomb of Infante Don Felipe. 1274. Marble. Villalcázar de Sirga (Palencia)*

72 *(Facing) "La Preciosa." Door of the chapter house in the Cathedral of Pamplona. Fourteenth century*

preserved many examples of this art, in which the expressive and stylistic elements are in perfect balance. Increasing naturalism could not destroy this rigorous order. The tracery of the arches and the exquisite floral motifs are in intimate harmony with the reliefs and effigies, and the bare surface against which all are set off. Most of the work from central Spain betrays the influence of important centers like Burgos and León, but also reflects the life of the local workshops with their varying tastes and customs.

During the fourteenth century, Asturias and Galicia developed a very characteristic style, marked by a distinct preference for a geometric, almost schematic treatment of masses. Examples of this art are found in the tomb of Fernán Pérez de Andrade at Betanzos and in the Cathedral of Orense. The archaism is sometimes less of a

stylistic tendency than a return to popular forms, as in the sculpture of the main door of the collegiate church of Toro. Other work displays greater refinement, for example, the intensely imaginative decoration of the Door of the Apostles in Avila cathedral.

In the course of the thirteenth and fourteenth centuries the Cathedral of Toledo was embellished with numerous pieces of sculpture. Among the more ancient of these, the best are the royal effigies in the presbytery, which date from the years between 1289 and 1308. The profuse and decidedly realistic reliefs of the Clock Door were carved toward the end of the thirteenth century. The decoration of the three doors of the west front belongs to the first half of the fourteenth century. That in the center is called the "Puerta del perdón" and the

73 *Master Bartomeu. Virgin and Child. Main door, Cathedral of Tarragona. Thirteenth century*

tympanum shows St. Ildefonsus receiving the chasuble. The side doors were carved in the workshop of the master responsible for the reliefs of the Puerta del perdón. The sculpture is the finest in Toledo and reveals a subtle balance between the Gothic of Reims and Italian formalism, both in spirit and in the simplicity of the masses, though this does not preclude a fitting sense of narrative.

The art of the fifteenth century is distinctly more courtly and graceful and places as much stress on capturing what is seen as on fidelity of conception. It is also well represented in Toledo cathedral, particularly in the admirable tombs of Archbishop Juan de Cerezuela (died 1442) and Pedro de Luna (died 1414). This art, influenced by the Burgundian school, eventually spread to the north. Evidence of

74 Guillermo Morey. Head of Countess Erme-sindis. Fourteenth century. Marble. Cathedral of Gerona

75 (Left) Guillermo Sagrera. *Archangel. Main door, "La Lonja" of Palma (Majorca). Fifteenth century. Stone*

76 (Right) *Detail of the tomb of Martín Vázquez de Arce. Fifteenth century. Marble. Cathedral of Sigüenza (Guadalajara)*

this is to be found in the tomb of the knight Gomez Carrillo de Acuña in Sigüenza cathedral, and in other monuments of a similar character.

In Navarre, the fourteenth century saw the development of a sculptural style of great interest and purity, which, though clearly influenced by Burgos and León, shows signs of direct contact with France. Perhaps the most ancient carvings in this style are those in the porch of Santa Maria la Real de Olite, which date from about 1300. The Cathedral of Pamplona possesses the most important body of sculpture of this kind. Work of great refinement, in which the French influence is clearly expressed, it includes the statues and reliefs of the doorway leading from the refectory to the cloister, carved sometime before 1330, and culminates in the door of the chapter house, called "La Preciosa" (Plate 72). Pamplona cathedral also treasures numerous early fifteenth-century carvings that reflect an advance toward the greater naturalism of Burgundian art. The foremost of these are the

work of French sculptors. This is true of the admirable epiphany group in the cloister, carved by Jacques Perut near the close of the fourteenth century. Among the various important fifteenth-century funerary monuments is the splendid tomb of King Charles the Noble and his wife, which was executed in 1416 by Janin Lomme of Tournai.

One of the major achievements of fourteenth-century sculpture in Navarre is the west front of the church of the Holy Sepulcher at Estella. Here the decoration is stylistically related to that of Santa Maria de Olite, as far as the treatment of the jambs is concerned, though the carvings of the tympanum and lintel are derived from the Preciosa door of Pamplona cathedral.

The Basque provinces have several admirable fourteenth-century porches. The most ancient of these, part of the church of San Pedro de Vitoria, is decorated with vigorously carved statuary, dating from about 1300, that still retains something of the spirit of Amiens.

In Catalonia, Gothic sculpture begins with Master Bartomeu, author of the marble statue of the Virgin on the center pier of the main porch of Tarragona cathedral (ca. 1277). This extraordinarily delicate figure is carved in a style that can best be described as idealized archaism (Plate 73). During the early part of the fourteenth century, another sculptor with a distinctive personality, Pedro Bonull, was active in the same region. In 1314 he carved the tomb of James II and Blanche of Anjou in the monastery of Santas Creus.

In Lérida, French and Italian influence overlapped, though in the magnificent wooden sculpture from Tredós (Barcelona Museum) and in the figure of St. Paul of Narbonne at Anglesola the Italian style is uppermost. The splendid tombs of the counts of Urgel, on the other hand, like the tomb of Armengol VII, built by Armengol X (died 1314) shortly before his own death, are obviously closer to the French (The Cloisters, New York).

We know the names and some of the work of an interesting group of Catalan sculptors active during the fourteenth century and the first half of the fifteenth. Jaime Cascalls completed the retable of Cornellá de Conflent in 1345 and, from 1360, served as master sculptor at the Cathedral of Lérida. Pedro Moragues, born about 1330, lived in Saragossa, where he carved the admirable tomb of Archbishop Lope Fernández de Luna (1381–1382) which adorns St. Michael's Chapel in the cathedral. Guillermo Morey is the author of noble monuments to Count Ramón Berenguer II and his wife, Ermesindis, who were buried in Gerona cathedral (Plate 74). Another member of the group, Pedro Ça Anglada, was employed on the stonework of the choir in Barcelona cathedral and is responsible for the beautiful figure of an angel over the door of the town hall, executed in 1406.

The finest of the Catalan sculptors of the fifteenth century, however, was Pedro Johan, who carved the outer door of the Palace of the Deputies in Barcelona. Between 1426 and 1433, the same artist executed the alabaster reliefs of the retable of Tarragona cathedral, which is noted for its pictorial and narrative qualities.

In Gerona, Burgundian Gothic is splendidly represented by the magnificent tomb of Bishop Bernardo de Pau (died 1457). In Majorca, the sculpture of the Portal del Mirador in Palma cathedral, begun in 1389 by Pedro Morey, is also worthy of attention. Some of the most distinguished Majorcan work of the fifteenth century was done by the sculptor and architect Guillermo Sagrera, who built the "Lonja" of Palma. In one of the doorways of this edifice stands the splendid figure of an archangel, revealing an extraordinary mastery of technique and a concept of form that owes something to the German as well as the Burgundian spirit (Plate 75).

The Burgundian tendencies, so conspicuous in the Spanish sculpture of about 1400, were displaced some sixty years later by the powerful Northern influences responsible for the origin of the Hispano-Flemish style. The chief characteristics of the latter, which became centered in Toledo and Burgos, are an increasing naturalism, combined with a strangely mannered conception of form, and a taste for ornament that finds expression in an emphasis on detail and in a persistent endeavor to reproduce in stone embroideries, jewelry, and the texture of fabrics. Prominent German and Flemish artists contributed to its rapid expansion, one of its first manifestations being the Door of the Lions in Toledo cathedral, chiefly the work of Juan Alemán.

The development of Hispano-Flemish sculpture was strongly influenced by the work of two brothers, Egas and Hanequín Cueman of Brussels, both of whom were in Toledo in 1458. The tombs in the monastery of Guadalupe, carved by Egas Cueman, reveal a novel conception of space and mass.

77 *Lorenzo Mercadente. The Nativity. Fifteenth century. Terra cotta. Puerta del Nacimiento, Cathedral of Seville*

Toledan Hispano-Flemish spread rapidly through central Spain and on into the northwest. It is characterized as much by the marked ornamentalism of its forms as by the simplicity of its masses and its human sentiment. The principal Spanish exponent of this style was the sculptor Sebastián de Almonacid, whose name first appears in 1486. He is the author of the double tomb of the Constable Alvaro de Luna and his wife in Toledo cathedral, and is thought to have carved the tomb of Martin Vázquez de Arce in Sigüenza cathedral (Plate 76). The idealized realism of the effigy is one of the supreme achievements of Spanish plastic art.

From about 1470 Gil de Siloé, a notable sculptor, probably of

142

Flemish origin, was the central figure of the Burgos school. He is known for his elaborate detail, bringing to his carving the delicacy of a goldsmith. The handsome effects he was able to obtain would be almost barbaric were it not for the heightened naturalism of his figures and his refined conception of space. His more important works include the funerary statues of King John II and his wife, Isabella of Portugal, in the Carthusian monastery of Miraflores, executed in 1486, the great retable in the same monastery, carved between 1496 and 1499, and the tombs of the Infante Alfonso and Juan de Padilla.

Lorenzo Mercadante of Brittany, who appeared in Seville in 1451, is an important figure in the area of pure sculpture. He executed a number of free-standing statues for the two doors of the cathedral known as the Puerta del Nacimiento and the Puerta del Bautismo, working in terra cotta, a material he handled with remarkable virtuosity, allied with great depth of feeling and tender humanity (Plate 77). His art exerted a natural influence on the religious sculptors of Andalusia, especially on Pedro Millán, who worked in Seville between 1487 and 1507.

In Spain, the Gothic period closes with a series of enormous sculptured retables, or shelves above the altar, a direct consequence of the work of Siloé and the Colonias. Uniformity is avoided by varying the rhythm of the compositions, grouping them differently, and contrasting them with the canopies over the scenes and figures. One of the best retables is that in Toledo cathedral. This was begun in 1502 by Diego Copín de Holanda, and finished by Sebastián de Almonacid.

In Castile, we should also mention the alabaster retables of the monastery of Paular (Madrid). The great retable of the Cathedral of Seville, in Andalusia, has thirty-five compartments filled with sculptures and reliefs. Work was done on this retable between 1482 and 1526. This huge undertaking, like others of the same kind, must have required collaboration among a number of workshops.

Overleaf 78:

Panel from the tomb of Don Sancho Saiz de Carrillo, Mahamud (Burgos). c.1300. Museum of Ancient Art, Barcelona

144

145

FOURTEENTH- AND FIFTEENTH-CENTURY PAINTING

In Spain the history of Gothic painting roughly coincides with the fourteenth and fifteenth centuries. This span of two hundred years can be divided into periods which correspond to four distinct styles, linear, Italo-Gothic, International Gothic, and Hispano-Flemish. The linear style, which has certain affinities with the late Romanesque, lasted until the middle of the fourteenth century. Italo-Gothic, as its name suggests, was strongly influenced by the schools of Italy, particularly those of Florence and Siena. International Gothic, introduced toward the end of the fourteenth century, is more mature and naturalistic, drawing most of its inspiration from France. The Hispano-Flemish style, which emerged during the second half of the fifteenth century, flourished mainly in Andalusia and Castile.

A remarkable feature of the evolution of Gothic painting in Spain is the extraordinary continuity of the Catalan school. Throughout the fourteenth century and the first half of the fifteenth, the Catalan painters preserved an impressive unity of style, one master succeeding the other without interruption. We know the names of many of the artists and a good deal about their work. In northern, western, and central Spain, on the other hand, progress was intermittent, depending on the appearance of individuals distinguished enough to establish a school. Some of these artists were foreigners, but their history shows that they were soon assimilated into Spanish life, acquiring a full share of the national characteristics, both good and bad. They had a predilection for the emotional aspects of the scenes they painted and displayed more interest in narration than in seeking formal beauty or technical perfection. In their later stages of development some of these artists schematized their figures to the point of expressionism.

Whereas frescoes formed the backbone of Romanesque painting, most Gothic painters worked on wooden panels. Nevertheless, some churches have mural paintings in chapels or cloister galleries. The

79 *Johannes Oliveri. The Road to Calvary. Mural from the refectory of the Cathedral of Pamplona. 1330. Museum of Navarre*

80   Panel from the tomb of Don Sancho Saiz de Carrillo, Mahamud (Burgos). c.1300. Museum of Ancient Art, Barcelona

81   (Facing) Detail of a retable given to the monastery of Quejana (Alava) by Pedro López de Ayala. 1396. Art Institute of Chicago

retables were large constructions built to support a series of vertical compositions. These retables were painted in tempera or in oils on a wooden panel prepared with a coat of gesso. The color scale is richer and more varied than that of the Romanesque, and commonly includes vermilion, cadmium, violet, green, lilac, ocher, white, gray, and yellow. The backgrounds of the retables and decorative elements, such as mullions, friezes, and canopies, are gilded, punched, or faced with ornamental plaster. Hence their sumptuous appearance and curious combination of elegance and unwordly idealism.

The Gothic era produced many triptychs, small paintings on wood and canvas, and articles of furniture with paintings on the inside. Miniaturists were also active, particularly during the thirteenth and

fourteenth centuries. In the fifteenth century, however, the discovery, first of the woodcut, and then of printing led to a gradual decline in the production of illuminated books.

The Linear Style

This style is remarkable for its subtlety. It is characterized, particularly in northern Spain, by undulating rhythms and a refined color scale. The backgrounds, in which architecture, furniture, and occasionally utensils are schematically represented, are in monochrome, but the figures that occupy the foreground have an expressive humanity, very different from the hieratic formalism of the past. A typical and very ancient example of the calligraphic style is the decoration of the tomb of Don Sancho Saiz de Carrillo (Barcelona Museum). This comes from Mahamud (Burgos) and marks the beginning of the Gothic style in Castile (Plates 78 and 80). It appears to be exactly contemporary with the interesting murals in one of the chapels in the Old Cathedral of Salamanca, executed in 1300 and designed by Anton Sánchez de Segovia.

One of the foremost masters of the linear style is Johannes Oliveri, a painter of Navarre. In 1330 he signed and dated the painting on the wall of the refectory of Pamplona cathedral, now in the Museum of Navarre (Plate 79). In this strikingly intense design the artist has been wholly successful in releasing the expressive power of linear rhythms. One is continuously aware of his efforts to tell a moving story, without departing from the formal conventions of his day. Other mural painters of Navarre share the same spirit, among them Roque de Artajona and the Master of Olite, who decorated the church of San Pedro de Olite around 1350. In Navarre, this style of panel painting persisted throughout the fourteenth century, as may be seen in the retable (Plate 81) that Pedro López de Ayala gave the monastery of Quejana in 1396 (Art Institute of Chicago).

Around 1300, in Catalonia, the calligraphic style gave an important demonstration of its narrative powers, particularly in the murals of the Old Cathedral of Lérida, in which a taste for anecdote is combined with a curious formalism, and in the mural decorations of Santo Domingo de Puigcerdá. Other regions of Spain possess interesting specimens of the same art, for example, the murals of the churches of Daroca, so strongly reminiscent of the Romanesque.

Italian Influence

The Italo-Gothic style, which arose in Catalonia during the second quarter of the fourteenth century, is characterized by balanced forms and a grave mannerism. Figures are painted against monochrome or gold backgrounds in a formula that barely hints at a third dimension. The style was introduced by Ferrer Bassa of Barcelona, a miniaturist and painter in the service of Alfonso IV and Pedro IV of Aragon. His known works cover the period from 1324 to his death in 1348. Most important are the murals of St. Michael's Chapel in the monastery of Pedralbes (Barcelona). Though clearly in the Gothic tradition, he departs from earlier practice by placing greater emphasis on the distribution of masses than on the play of lines. The rhythm that animates his forms is slow and restrained.

Bassa's style was fully developed by his own son, Arnaldo (Plate 82), and by Ramón Destorrents. Italo-Gothic was popularized by the Serra brothers, who dominated the Barcelona school during the second half of the fourteenth century. Working singly or together, they executed many fine retables, placing their somewhat shallow but not ungraceful lyricism at the service of the Gothic narrative taste. One of their nephews, Francisco Serra, established himself in Valencia, bringing with him the family style.

Barcelona was not the only Catalan city to accept new ideas from Italy. Sometimes these were received directly from Italian painters working in Spain, like Francesco d'Oberto, who was active in Tarragona about the middle of the fourteenth century. Juan of Tarragona was his most talented successor. In Lérida, the Italianizing trend first appears in the retable of San Vicente de Estopiñán.

International Gothic

International Gothic style is characterized by a growing interest in the representation of real environments and the possibilities of livelier

rhythms. Some of the sinuousness of linear Gothic was restored, though firmly subordinated to a new awareness of the natural model. Gold backgrounds lingered on only in the retables.

This style was brought to Catalonia by Luis Borrassá, a painter born in Gerona. In 1383 we find him settled in Barcelona. A master of stylization, Borrassá also possessed a strong and personal color sense, his palette betraying a fondness of lively reds and greens. These qualities are discernible even in the retable of the Archangel Gabriel (Cathedral, Barcelona), one of his more archaic works. His narrative range was greatly extended by his skill in manipulating space. This is particularly apparent in the scenes depicted in the retable of San Pedro de Tarrasa, painted in 1411 (Plate 84), and in the retable of Santa Clara (Museum, Vich). The International style spread rapidly through Catalonia. At the same time it flourished in Roussillon, Tarragona, and Lérida, as the result of Burgundian influence. Ramón de Mur and Mateo Ortoneda, who worked in Tarragona, and Jaime Ferrer of Lérida were all affected, to a greater or lesser degree, by Borrassá's example.

Borrassá was succeeded as central figure of the Barcelona school by Bernardo Martorell (died 1452), a painter in whom scrupulous attention to detail is combined with touches of poetry. In spite of the limitations of his empirical and conventional perspective, he was able to convey an impression of depth and space, and to give life to every element of his composition (Plate 86). One of the finest works of his early period is the retable of St. George (Louvre and Art Institute of Chicago), painted with extraordinary sensitivity and a subtle use of glazes. Martorell employed a color scale very different from that of Borrassá, preferring rare and delicate lilacs, violets, yellows, greenish grays, and whites to the vivid and even violent hues of the latter. A central position in the career of the artist is occupied by his only documented work, the retable of San Pedro de Pubol, commissioned in 1437. His last known project is the great retable of the Savior in Barcelona cathedral, which he completed shortly before his death.

82   Arnaldo Bassa. The Consecration of St. Marcus. Detail. c. 1350. Painted on panel. Cathedral of Manresa (Barcelona)

83   Master of the Privileges. Retable of St. Eulalia. Fourteenth century. Painted on panel. Cathedral of Palma (Majorca)

The spirit of refinement that illuminates his major works is equally evident in his miniatures. His influence extended far beyond his immediate circle of colleagues and disciples.

In the middle of the fourteenth century the Majorcan school fell under the influence of Catalan painting, without losing the contacts with Italy which had been so important during the previous fifty years. This period is chiefly characterized by the work of an anonymous miniaturist and painter of outstanding quality, known as the Master of the Privileges after he had illustrated the famous Majorcan

Book of Privileges of about 1334. He is also the author of the retable of St. Eulalia in Palma cathedral (Plate 83) and of another in Santa Quiteria. His style is related to the art of Pietro Lorenzetti and Duccio.

During the second half of the fourteenth century the Majorcan school included a number of interesting painters, in particular, Juan Daurer, the Mayol family, the Master of San Mateo, and Francisco Comes, an artist in whom archaizing elements contend with the realistic form and detail of the International Gothic. More important are two painters active about 1400, the Master of Santa Eulalia and the Master of Montesión. The former is the author of one of the most refined paintings of the Majorcan school, the Virgin of Slumber in Santa Eulalia de Palma. The Master of Montesión painted the well-preserved retable dedicated to the Virgin in the church of Montesión, in the same city. The style is strongly Italian, the drawing sober, precise, and elegant.

In Valencia, after an Italo-Gothic phase largely imposed by Francisco Serra (nephew of the Catalan painters Jaime and Pedro Serra), the International style began with great brilliance. It was encouraged by the considerable talents of artists like Lorenzo Zaragoza, an Aragonese by origin, whose works include the beautiful retable of Jérica (1394–1395), Pedro Nicolau, active around the turn of the century and author of the characteristic Coronation of the Virgin in the Cleveland Museum of Art (Plate 85), Miguel Alcañiz, whose Gospel scenes are so full of movement, and the lyric Gonzalo Peris, noted for the beauty of his saints and Virgins as well as for the sinuousness of his designs. The Barcelona Museum possesses one of his best paintings, the retable dedicated to St. Barbara.

However, the painter chiefly responsible for the transition from the style of the fourteenth to that of the fifteenth century, was Marçal de Sax, who was of German origin. The most important of his works to be preserved is the splendid retable of St. George, one of the treasures of the Victoria and Albert Museum in London (Plate 87). The central scene depicts the conquest of Valencia by James I of Aragon. A distinctive feature of the work of this artist is his great skill in composition. The figures are grouped with great freedom, but without loss of order or clarity and without sacrifice of detail. The battle scene is a careful study of the weapons and military pomp of the period. It is clear that the art of Marçal de Sax must have contributed heavily to the spread of International Gothic style in Valencia and the consequent abandonment of a tradition of static images and delicate, but ingenuous compositions.

The evolution toward methods of representation more effective than the images of the Italo-Gothic style, with their decidedly decorative flavor, is illustrated in the work of a number of interesting artists. Some of them we know by name, as Benito Arnaldín, and Nicolas Solana. Others remain anonymous, and, as usual, are identified by titles derived from the site of their most important works, like the masters of Retascón, Langa, and Lanaja.

At the heart of this movement, and its finest representative, was the painter Bonanat Zaortiga, who was active in Saragossa from about 1403. Several of Zaortiga's retables have been preserved, one of the best being that of the Virgin of Hope in Tudela cathedral. The carefully elaborated grouping and the sometimes almost aggressive primitivism of the details make his style an unusually striking one.

By 1400 International Gothic had spread, quite rapidly, though somewhat haphazardly, through the different regions of Spain, driving out the primitive ideas that even Italo-Gothic had largely retained. Excellent paintings in this style are to be found all the way from Navarre to Andalusia. The latter province, for example, has some beautiful studies of the Virgin, such as the Virgin of the Remedios (Cathedral of Seville), and the Virgin of Rocamador, preserved in the church of San Lorenzo in the same city.

In the broad regions of central Spain, Gothic painting of the pre-1450 period lacked Catalonia's close-knit organization of studios and skills that were often handed down from father to son. In Castile and León progress was almost always the result of the sudden emergence of an outstanding master who served as an inspiration to the local artists and craftsmen. In about 1379 the Florentine Gerardo Starnina painted the altarpiece of the Savior in Toledo cathedral, bringing to his work the clarity of form typical of Italian painting.

84 Luis Borrassá. Christ and St. Peter. 1411. Painted on panel. San Pedro de Tarrasa (Barcelona)

85 Pedro Nicolau. The Coronation of the Virgin. 1400. Painted on panel. Cleveland Museum of Art

Rodríguez of Toledo, who signed the frescoes in St. Blaise's Chapel in the same cathedral, begun in 1395, has obviously adapted Starnina's style to the prevailing Spanish taste. His hagiographic and Gospel scenes, arranged in two zones, cover the full width of the walls with massive and monumental forms. Rodríguez is also thought to be the author of the huge retable of Archbishop Sánchez de Rojas from the church of San Benito de Valladolid, now in the Prado. Its chief qualities are the naturalism of the figures and the relatively advanced treatment of space. An air of serene harmony pervades these compositions, from which every hint of drama has been banished.

The great retable in the Old Cathedral of Salamanca is perhaps the most important Spanish work of art to bear the marks of Italian influence. The impressiveness of this retable, with its fifty-three compartments, framing as many paintings, is further enhanced by a great series of frescoes covering the vault of the apse above. All this is the work of Dello di Niccolò Delli, referred to as Nicolas Florentino in the contract of 1445. In spite of the restrictions imposed by his subject and his obligation to retell each Gospel story in plain and concrete terms, Delli showed himself a skillful draftsman, capable of adding delicious poetic touches to the simple narrative vein. His extended range of forms and sinuous, varied rhythms are in the typical spirit of the International style. The most ambitious part of the work is undoubtedly the frescoes of the vault, where the problems are resolved with a combination of decorative feeling, brilliant rhythms, and splendid harmony.

In León, the International style was first introduced by a painter of great refinement, whose French origin is reflected in his name, Nicolás Francés. He was already living in León during the episcopate of Alfonso de Cusanza (1424–1437). In the cathedral records he is described as an artist in stained glass, though he is also the author of the great retable, executed in 1434. Nicolás Francés painted extensively and well. His work includes the mural decorations in the cloister and two compositions in the ambulatory of León cathedral, together with various paintings on wood, the best of which is in the Cincinnati Art Museum. His style appears to derive from that of the Paris school of the first quarter of the fifteenth century. In particular, he possesses the same subtlety of tone, the same grace in arranging the elements of his composition against a landscape background, and the same neatness of detail, but above all the same harmony of color. Until his death in 1468, he was for thirty years the foremost painter of the school of León, which also included followers such as Juan de Burgos, who signed his name to a small Annunciation now in the Fogg

Overleaf 86 and 87:

(Left) Bernardo Martorell. The Nativity. Detail. Fifteenth century. Painted on panel. Collection Lippmann, Berlin. (Right) Marçal de Sax. Retable of St. George. c. 1400. Painted on panel. Victoria and Albert Museum, London

161

Art Museum (Cambridge, Massachusetts), and the Master of Palan-
quinos, author of several paintings on wood.

Hispano-Flemish

Hispano-Flemish is a synthesis of International Gothic, in its Spanish
form, and the influence of the great Flemish masters of the fifteenth
century. The Hispano-Flemish style was prevalent throughout the
latter half of the fifteenth century, but its geographical penetration
was unequal and fluctuating. Thus, in Castile and León the influx of
new ideas from Flanders brought a lasting transformation in the art
of painting. In the states of Aragon, on the other hand, Hispano-
Flemish not only failed to make ground, but even provoked a reaction
toward Italianism and ultimately the Renaissance.

The Hispano-Flemish style is remarkable for its tendency toward
naturalism, its substitution of landscapes for the customary gold background, its interest in atmospheric values, and its use of oils rather
than tempera. Textures are carefully studied and faithfully reproduced. Details, even though simplified and poeticized, tend to be
taken from the real world.

Chronologically, the first exponent of the Hispano-Flemish style
was Luis Dalmau, a native of Valencia, who must have been born
around the year 1400. Though most of his work has been lost, the few
paintings that survive are of great significance. In 1445 he painted the
Retable of the Councillors, an altarpiece for the chapel of the municipal council of Barcelona (Plate 88). His technique, precise and painstaking, though not without brilliance and even inspiration, embodies
various elements adapted from Van Eyck. This painting, executed in
oils, has all the characteristics of the style it represents, including the
sensation of viewing the world through an optical instrument.

Dalmau's influence on the Catalan school of painting was short-
lived. A group that still clung to the gold backgrounds and narrative
tastes of the beginning of the century could not be expected to accept
the innovations of the Hispano-Flemish style without fear and hesita-
tion. In spite of this, primitivism was gradually overcome. The
essential step in this direction was taken by the painter Jaime Huguet
(1414–1492). Huguet was a sensitive painter, the creator of pro-

foundly human types, whose features and expressions produce an un-
forgettable effect. His figures, serene and grave, their gestures marked
by a spiritual elegance, are suffused with a singular idealism. Technically, from the almost miniaturistic scenes of the epiphany in the
Museum of Vich to the huge figures of the retable of St. Augustine
executed between 1465 and 1480 (Museum, Barcelona), the work of
this painter is a development of the formula evolved by Martorell.

The chef-d'œuvre of Huguet's first period is the altarpiece of
St. George, now in the Museum, Barcelona (Plate 89). During his
second period (1445–1448) he may have been influenced by Dalmau's technical innovations, but these he soon renounced in favor of
his own method of working. The third period (1454–1465) is that of
full maturity and is marked by works as splendid as the retable of
Sarriá, showing St. Vincent at the stake, in the Barcelona Museum,
and that of the SS. Abdón and Sennen (1459–1460), preserved in the
church of Santa Maria in Tarrasa. In these paintings the sumptuousness and ultra-refinement of the colors are a sign of Huguet's advance
toward the new culture of the Renaissance. Adjacent color zones have
their own modulations of light and shade that are never allowed to
become confused; the effect is grandiose, but never harsh.

The Hispano-Flemish style reached Majorca with Pedro Nisart,
perhaps the most outstanding personality of the period. He is the author
of the altarpiece of St. George in the Diocesan Museum of Palma,
commissioned in 1468 (Plate 90). This work is said to be based on a
lost painting by Van Eyck, once in the possession of Alfonso the Mag-
nanimous.

The final form of Majorcan Gothic is the creation of other painters,
who displayed more sympathy for the Italian style and Huguet's
humanism than for the premises of Hispano-Flemish. This is true of
the Master of Las Predelas, and even more so of Martín Torner and

Overleaf 88 and 89:

*(Left) Luis Dalmau. Detail of the Retable of the Councillors. 1445. Painted on
panel. Museum of Ancient Art, Barcelona. (Right) Jaime Huguet. St. George.
Detail. 1459–1460, Painted on panel. Museum of Ancient Art, Barcelona*

Pedro Terrencs, both of whom were influenced by Alonso de Sedano.

Strangely enough, Castile, which had the oldest and firmest relations with Flanders, was the last to receive the new ideas that were to crystallize in the Hispano-Flemish style. The chief contribution in this direction was made by a painter known to history as Jorge Inglés. In 1455 he was engaged in painting a magnificent altarpiece of the Virgin for the hospital of Buitrago (now in the collection of the Duque del Infantado). The donor, whom the artist shows kneeling at the Virgin's feet, was Don Iñigo López de Mendoza, marquis of Santillana, a poet and one of the richest and most important men of his age. In these paintings a vigorous handling of space and realistic portraiture go hand in hand with a keen awareness of the tactile qualities and texture of the materials: velvets, brocades, and metals.

Jorge Inglés, as his name implies, was an Englishman, or possibly a Fleming, who had settled in Spain. His career is typical of that curious process of assimilation so frequently experienced by the foreign painters who came to Spain and made their home there. The lyrical refinement of his earlier work gradually gives way to an overriding concern for narration and feeling that borders on expressionism. This artist is also regarded as the author of the altarpiece of San Jerónimo de la Mejorada (Provincial Museum, Valladolid), and of a picture in which a saint is shown preaching, now in the Cincinnati Art Museum (Plate 91).

One of the greatest of the Castilian painters to adopt the Hispano-Flemish style was Fernando Gallego, who was active, mainly in Salamanca, approximately between 1466 and 1506. There are certain resemblances between Gallego's paintings and those of Dierik Bouts, although the former's types are decidedly Spanish. Gallego was primarily interested in achieving a convincing representation of space, arranging his figures with a certain freedom, though still with Gothic angularity (Plate 92). He had that sculptural conception of form that leads to close and intensive modeling and that has long been one of the hallmarks of Spanish painting.

90 Pedro Nisart. Retable of St. George. 1468. Painted on panel. Diocesan Museum, Palma (Majorca)

91 (Left) Jorge Inglés. Saint Preaching. 1455. Painted on panel. Cincinnati Art Museum

92 (Right) Fernando Gallego. Epiphany. c. 1480. Painted on panel. Museum of Art, Toledo

The earliest of Gallego's altarpieces is that of San Ildefonso in Zamora cathedral, an oil painting made about 1466, in which bright colors are combined with subtle grays. In about 1470 he painted the altarpiece of the Virgin, St. Andrew, and St. Christopher for the Old Cathedral of Salamanca, and the Pietà in the Prado Museum, both of which he signed. In these paintings we are strongly aware of his interest in sculptural modeling and in the rendering of different textures.

In the period between 1480 and 1490 he completed some very important projects, in which he was forced to enlist the aid of assistants. This, a common enough occurrence in medieval Spain, owing to the vast amount of work commissioned by patrons and donors, resulted in some distortion of his style. His chief assistant was a Francisco Gallego, who may have been his brother. The finest works of this period are the altarpiece from Ciudad Rodrigo, now in the University Art Gallery, Tucson, Arizona, and that painted for Zamora cathedral between 1496 and 1506. At the same time, we should not forget a work by Gallego that stands apart, both in subject and in technique, from all those mentioned above. This is the ceiling of the library of the University of Salamanca, painted between 1473 and 1494. Here Gallego used tempera for the blue backgrounds and oils for the signs of the zodiac and personifications of the planets.

In some instances, the task of painting narrative scenes and sacred images to fill the several compartments of a retable was entrusted to two or more painters. This is true of the retable of the Luna Chapel in Toledo cathedral, an excellent example of the Hispano-Flemish style. The contract of 1488 mentions the names of two artists, Juan de Segovia and Sancho de Zamora. The latter may perhaps be identical with the Master of San Ildefonso, one of the most characteristic figures of the last phase of the Gothic. Without relinquishing the spiritual qualities expressed in the angularity of the style or the legacy of a centuries-old tradition, he managed to imbue his work with true human feeling. To this painter we owe the panels showing St. Anastasius and St. Louis, in the Provincial Museum of Valladolid, and the panel of San Ildefonso receiving the chasuble, in the Louvre, in which smooth modeling proves perfectly compatible with a sharp delineation of form.

These were not the only talented artists at work in Castile and León during the last third of the fifteenth century. Another painter of note was the Master of Avila, who carried expressionism even further than Gallego, combining it with foreshortening to achieve some unusual effects, which nevertheless remain compatible with a notable precision of composition and form. His finest work is the Nativity in the Lázaro Galdiano Museum, Madrid, which forms part of a triptych.

The extent to which certain Spanish painters of the late fifteenth century assimilated typically Flemish characteristics is illustrated by Diego de la Cruz. His most distinctive qualities are skillful execution, a distaste for expressionistic narrative with its attendant distortions, a sweetness that does not detract from the intensity of the forms, and a gift for balancing groups of figures against their surroundings and in space. Diego's personality is revealed by a signed panel in Palencia. His most important work is the great altarpiece of the Catholic Kings, now divided among several museums in the United States.

There can be no doubt about the extent of Diego's influence during the last fifteen years of the fifteenth century. Of his immediate followers the most important were the Master of Los Balbases and the Master of Burgos. The work of the latter represents an evolution toward an Italian style more in keeping with the ideas being advanced in Spain shortly before the year 1500.

In the last quarter of the fifteenth century the Hispano-Flemish style reached Andalusia, where its features were somewhat modified to suit the softer temperament of the south. The principal schools were those of Seville and Cordova. The former included a number of interesting artists, among them Antón and Diego Sánchez, who signed the Road to Calvary now in the Fitzwilliam Museum, Cambridge (England), and Pedro Sánchez, author of the Entombment now in the Budapest Museum.

The central personality of the Cordovan school was the painter Pedro of Cordova, who in 1475 signed the great panel of the Annunciation in the cathedral of that city. His style is related to that of the schools of southern France, but its essential Spanishness is apparent in the sculptural modeling of the forms and the ornamentalism of the details. Andalusian imagination, grace, and elegance find expression in his treatment of space. The middle ground is occupied by the figures of the Virgin and the archangel in dazzling brocades, the background by a suite of rooms gleaming with tiles, and the foreground by a series of eight figures, separated from the middle zone by the baroque tracery of a balustrade. Well-studied lighting effects add to the beauty of this original painting, in which ochers and carmines predominate.

One of the leading Spanish artists of the last third of the fifteenth century was Bartolomé Bermejo. The signature "Bartolomeus Vermeio Cordubensis" on the Pietà in Barcelona cathedral, one of his later works, completed in 1490, indicates that he was born in Cordova. At the same time, there is nothing in the Andalusian art of that period to explain the origin of his style or the source of his technique. We believe that Bermejo must have studied in Flanders, perhaps in direct contact with Dierik Bouts (1420–1475), with whom he has certain stylistic affinities. In spite of this Flemish training, Bermejo's work leaves us in no doubt concerning his Spanish origin. Robust, virile, and dramatic, it is characterized by a profound gravity, the counterpart of the lyrical refinement so typical of the Spanish genius (Plate 93).

The career of the artist is roughly marked out by the traces of his influence and a few recorded dates. Restless by temperament, he worked in various centers, the chief of these being Valencia, where he painted an admirable St. Michael, originally intended for Tous and now in the collection of Lady Ludlow (England). This is an intensely stylized work with accurately rendered textures, marvelously decorative by virtue of its color harmonies and rhythms. The portrait of the kneeling donor is a powerful affirmation of that celebrated Spanish realism, of which Bermejo was to provide other splendid examples. The center panel of an altarpiece of the Virgin now in Acqui (Italy) is evidently of later date. The background is a beautifully observed landscape, but the chief interest of the painting lies in the strong sculptural modeling of the figures.

Between 1474 and 1477 Bermejo must have worked in Aragon, on the altarpiece of Santa Engracia, originally in Daroca and now divided

93 *Bartolomé Bermejo. The Descent into Hell. Detail. c.1480. Painted on panel. Institute of Hispanic Art, Barcelona*

among various collections, and on the impressive altarpiece of St. Dominic of Silos, now in the Prado Museum. His influence is apparent in the work of Martín Bernat, Miguel Ximénez, and other Aragonese artists. In 1486 Bemejo was in Barcelona. The Pietà, already mentioned, was painted in 1490. That this is a work of Bermejo's maturity is clear both from the inimitable quality of the background landscape, with its grazing light, advanced naturalism, and spatial freedom, and from the dramatic severity both of the figures and of the atmosphere that surrounds them.

The Gothic style and an essentially medieval, narrative naturalism continued to characterize Castilian painting until well into the sixteenth century. This survival of archaic formulas is partially attributable to certain painters of foreign origin, for example, the Flemish painter known as Juan of Flanders, who from 1496 was employed in the service of Isabella of Castile. This artist was the author of a handsome portable altarpiece. The various miniatures of which it was composed are now dispersed, some to the Royal Palace in Madrid and others to various collections in Europe and America. Juan of Flanders remained essentially an expressionist painter beneath the virtuosity of his Flemish technique.

After the death of the Queen of Castile in 1504, Juan worked in Salamanca and Palencia, where he died in about 1519. During this last period of his life he painted altarpieces for the University of Salamanca, for the cathedral, and for the church of San Lázaro in the city of Palencia. These paintings, the size of which must have appeared excessive to an artist with notions of space derived from a fifteenth-century Flemish training, are a tribute to his versatility. The change of scale and the rapidity of execution, required by local circumstances, obliged the artist to create a new style, in which he releases, in surprising form, the expressionism that lurked behind the scrupulous technique characteristic of the paintings of his youth.

Pedro Berruguete

Among the painters whose style may be regarded as transitional between Gothic and Renaissance, the foremost is undoubtedly Pedro Berruguete, a native of Paredes de Nava in the province of Palencia.

94   Pedro Berruguete. Federigo di Montefeltro and his Son. c. 1480. Ducal Palace, Urbino

His pre-eminence derives from the eclecticism and the spirit of humanity that permeate his art. Even during his apprenticeship, Berruguete had to struggle to master a number of divergent influences. After an early period in Flanders, or in the profoundly Flemish atmosphere of the Castilian Gothic, he went to Italy, where he remained for several years. These different elements of his training, perfectly assimilated by his unusually receptive, but stoutly Spanish nature, led him to a style rooted in Gothic ideals and Gothic forms, but Renaissance in the warmth of its humanism. Renaissance characteristics are more apparent in the work of Berruguete's Italian period. His later painting reveals a certain progression toward a Hispano-Flemish Gothicism.

The first historical references to Berruguette relate to his stay at

Urbino. The great *condottiere,* Federigo di Montefeltro, duke of Urbino, had summoned Joos van Gent to decorate the library and study of his magnificent palace with allegories of the liberal arts and portraits of Biblical and pagan thinkers. Berruguete may have collaborated with him, but there is no doubt that the allegories and many of the more vigorous portraits of the series are by his hand alone (National Gallery, London, and the Louvre). He also painted the solemn portrait of Federigo and his son (Ducal Palace, Urbino), which gives some idea of his mastery of tactile values and of the airy qualities of physical space, perfectly suggested in depth (Plate 94). These paintings were all executed between 1480 and 1481. During his stay at Urbino, Berruguete completed a certain amount of work which has since remained in Italy. Moreover, he also painted the hands of the portrait of Montefeltro in the famous picture by Piero della Francesca in the Brera Gallery, Milan.

In 1483 Berruguete was busy in Toledo cathedral, working on the now-lost mural decoration of the cloister. Judging from its style the retable of Santa Eulalia in his native village must have been painted during the last ten years of the fifteenth century. Its narrative scenes, the naturalism of which reflects the life of contemporary Castile, gave the artist an opportunity to demonstrate his ability and the final victory over primitivism. The figures of kings and prophets on the predella establish Berruguete as the forerunner of the Spanish portraitists of the seventeenth century. His retable of St. John the Baptist, preserved in Santa Maria del Campo (Burgos), is impressive in the strength of the figures and the clarity of the construction, which lend the subject, by dint of realism, a surprising air of unreality. Even more important, as an ensemble, is the retable of St. Thomas in Avila, the best of its numerous scenes being the vision of the saint overcoming temptation. The persistence of the Gothic tradition is revealed in the free use of gold and the abundance of brocades.

We have cited only a few of Berruguete's numerous works. Hardly less important are the Annunciation in the Carthusian monastery of

95   *Pedro Berruguete. The Holy Family. Signed and dated 1500. Private collection, Paredes de Nava*

Miraflores, and the Holy Family signed and dated in 1500, now part of a private collection in Paredes de Nava (Plate 95). Berruguete's influence is strongly apparent in the work of various painters who were active in Castile and León during the first third of the sixteenth century.

APPLIED ARTS IN THE GOTHIC PERIOD

During the latter part of the Middle Ages, conditions strongly favored the growth and development of the applied arts. The little workshops that arose in the shadow of palaces, cathedrals, and monasteries transformed not only jewels, gold, and silver, but also modest household goods and simple utensils into works of art. It appears as if a sound aesthetic sense and refined taste had penetrated the very depths of the people's spirit. The most insignificant pieces of furniture and the humblest earthenware pots shared the same beauty as costly jewelry. The popular art of the thirteenth, fourteenth, and fifteenth centuries reached beyond its immediate iconographic or utilitarian purpose to the more exalted level of the creative arts.

Illuminated Manuscripts

The introduction of the linear style coincided with another important process begun during the final period of the Romanesque, the transfer of part of the work of the monastic scriptoria to lay miniaturists. The services of these artists were available not only to the cathedrals and religious communities, but also to the court, the nobility, and bibliophiles in general. The most important codices of the thirteenth century are the *libros Alfonsíes*, created under the direct influence of Alfonso the Wise. Among these, the finest are the *Cantigas* (Escorial Library, National Library of Florence, National Library of

96 Page from the Cantigas de Alfonso el Sabio (Canticles of Alfonso the Wise). *Thirteenth century. Library of the Escorial, Madrid*

178

Como caeu o mastro da galea e matou o Almiral

E quisto sou libres no primo filho que offereu ant villas

Como os mercadores empregaron todo seu auer en laa

Como os mercadores fezeron meter a laa na nave

E leixou pelo mar ferir consigo e naueg meron a laa e al
no fargou

Como tornar u eran a sa filla e toveu o muito de seu auer

Madrid), manuscripts profusely illustrated with scenes of an anecdotal and narrative character, depicting men of every social condition and a wide range of medieval backgrounds (Plate 96). The work of a number of miniaturists, they are remarkable for their wit and gay coloring.

During the fourteenth century the miniaturists produced numerous manuscripts on profane and religious themes; some of these were of outstanding artistic merit, particularly the *Chronicle of Troy*, the *Dominical Oscense*, the *Breviary of King Martin*, and the Valencia *Missal*. The *Missal of St. Eulalia* in Barcelona cathedral contains an admirable version of the Last Judgment (Plate 97). Dating from 1403, it is the work of Rafael Destorrents. The so-called Bible of Alba, completed in 1430, is an important fifteenth-century volume with paintings by various artists, some of them Jews. During the later Middle Ages, many of the painters who enjoyed the patronage of the royal courts of Aragón and Castile or the protection of the more powerful nobles were also miniaturists. This is true of Destorrents, Arnau de la Pena, and Bernardo Martorell in Catalonia, and of Jorge Inglés and Nicolás Francés in Castile. Several magnificent libraries were formed, the finest being those of King John II of Castile, the Duke of Béjar, Don Alvaro de Luna, and Don Iñigo López de Mendoza, marquis of Santillana.

In spite of increasing competition from prints, which from the fourteenth century (and especially from the last third of the fifteenth, with the introduction of the printing press) had been gradually asserting themselves as the principal medium for the diffusion of iconography, pages of manuscripts continued to be ornamented with large illustrations and decorative initials right up to the sixteenth century. This late period produced some magnificent examples of the miniaturist's art in its Books of Hours, Choir Books, and Missals. Its masterpieces include the *Book of Hours* of the Royal Chapel of Granada, and the *Misal Rico* of Cisneros. The churches of Seville, Granada, Guadalupe, and Avila possess fine collections of anthem books.

97   *Rafael Destorrents. Page from the* Missal of St. Eulalia. *1403. Cathedral of Barcelona*

Goldsmiths and Silversmiths

Spain is a country rich in religious goldsmith's and silversmith's work, the later Middle Ages and the first half of the sixteenth century being particularly well represented. The most primitive work of the Gothic period is closely related to sculpture. The thirteenth-century pieces are strongly reminiscent of the Romanesque, but in the fourteenth century the Gothic style rose to a high degree of purity.

The supreme achievment is the silver altar of Gerona cathedral, which was begun by Master Bartomeu in 1320. In the middle of the century it was enlarged with a new series of silver and enamel reliefs centered upon the image of the Virgin. This bears the signature of the famous goldsmith Pere Berneç, whose name occurs in historical documents between the years 1345 and 1380. The altar is surmounted by a superb baldachin, also worked in silver, an outstanding example of mid-fourteenth-century craftsmanship. The ensemble is one of the finest pieces of medieval metalwork in Europe. The processional crosses, reliquaries, chalices, and other liturgical objects preserved in large quantities in the cathedrals and churches of Spain are further evidence of the high level of artistry achieved by the Gothic goldsmith.

The Arfe family, whose name is derived from that of their native village, Harff near Cologne, were goldsmiths of genius who worked in Spain during the early part of the sixteenth century. Enrique de Arfe was the author of a number of admirable monstrances—among the most important of their kind—including that of the monastery of Sahagún in León, that of Cordova cathedral, and, above all, that of Toledo cathedral, a marvelous piece of frankly transitional design. The lightness of its architectural forms in silvergilt and the splendid proportions of all its elements proclaim it a masterpiece (Plate 98).

The craftsmen of the Gothic period also worked in other metals, less noble than gold and silver but just as capable of yielding an aesthetic effect. The chief of these was iron, with which they made candelabra, ornamental locks and handles, knockers, fittings for chests and other pieces of furniture, lecterns, weapons, and, above all, superb chapel grilles for the churches. Heavy wrought-iron grilles were also used in civil buildings, like the famous House of the Shells in Salamanca. Other craftsmen worked in brass, copper, and bronze, producing elegant crosses, lamps, jugs, and other objects, religious and profane. These metals were almost always gilded, and sometimes engraved or embellished with enameled silver plaques or rough rubies.

Ceramics, Embroidery, and Furniture

The most important characteristic of Spanish ceramics during the Gothic period is the persistence of Moorish designs and techniques. The rhythms, colors, and other qualities are derived from those created in centers dominated by Moorish culture. The gold lusterware of Manises, the green and violet earthenware of Paterna and Teruel, and the *azulejos* (glazed earthenware plaques) of Toledo and Seville retained their pre-eminence until Renaissance forms were introduced.

Then the delicate, repetitive motifs, inscriptions and allegorical figures gave way to large figural compositions, grotesques or ornamental motifs like urns, garlands, and such. A monument with ceramic decoration that deserves special mention is the tomb of Don Leon Enríquez in Santa Paula of Seville. The Renaissance style was introduced to Seville by Francisco Niculoso de Pisa, noted chiefly for his altarpiece in the chapel of the Alcazar Real. In about 1500 the first pieces were fired in the kilns of Talavera de la Reina. These were frankly Renaissance in style.

As for glassware, special interest attaches to that produced in Catalonia during the later Middle Ages and the sixteenth century; it is based on the work of the masters from Murano. Elegant decoration in color and refined forms are the characteristics of this art, which gradually became more baroque as the subtlety of its technique and the variety of its forms and ornament increased.

Among the examples of minor arts of the fourteenth and fifteenth centuries, pride of place must go to the liturgical embroideries. Altar frontals of high artistic quality are preserved in the Museum of Vich, the monastery of Guadalupe (Plate 99), and in Tarragona cathedral, though perhaps the most notable is that dedicated to St. George in the Palace of the Deputies in Barcelona. These frontals, like certain embroidered altars, are thoroughly pictorial in their effect, the figures composing animated narrative scenes with themes drawn from the Gospels and the lives of the saints. Silks, velvets, and brocades were imported from the Moorish centers of Spain as well as from Italy. During the late Middle Ages, Granada, Almería, Toledo, and Valencia were the cities best known for their artistic textiles. Another important product was tooled leather, likewise influenced by Moorish techniques and Nasrid work. The Royal Armory of Madrid has an admirable leather shield bearing the arms of Ribera and Mendoza.

The furniture of the Gothic period is modeled on its architecture, both in form and in decoration. The commonest decorative elements are tracery, fenestrations, and openwork wheels; these alternate with carved figures, particularly in the choir stalls, which are really as much sculpture as furniture. There are choir stalls of this kind in the cathedrals of Toledo, Barcelona, Palencia, and León, as well as other fine work on which the furniture-makers collaborated with eminent sculptors such as Rodrigo Alemán and Pere Ça Anglada. During the Plateresque period, furniture tended to be as profusely decorated as the façades of the buildings. Italian types, like the desk and the monk's armchair, were adapted to Spanish tastes and acquired certain very characteristic features, thanks either to Mudejar influence or the simplification of the decoration.

The sixteenth-century Spanish *bargueño* or painted desk is a conversation piece. Caskets, coffers, and large chests were often richly ornamented with carvings and metal facings. In the time of the Catholic Kings, the painted or carved wooden caskets of the Gothic period were succeeded by velvet ones with gold-enameled fittings. Caskets inlaid with ivory and bone and decorated with Mudejar motifs are also very typical and continued to be made through the centuries.

100 (Left) Tower of the church of El Salvador (Teruel). Mudejar architecture. Fourteenth century

101 (Right) Patio of the Palace of Alfonso XI, Tordesillas (Valladolid). c.1340

MOORISH TRADITION AND MUDEJAR STYLE

The word Mudejar comes from the Arabic *mudayan* meaning "subjugated." Thus, Mudejar art is the art of the Mohammedans who were permitted to remain on Christian territory. The progress of the reconquest, from the taking of Toledo in 1085 to the occupation of Seville in 1248, resulted in numerous important centers of Islamic culture falling into Christian hands. In these centers age-old traditions and standards were stubbornly maintained, thanks largely to the strong aesthetic support received from the Moorish Kingdom of Granada. At the same time, the development of Mudejar art was favored by medieval religious tolerance. In the reconquered cities, Mohammedans, Jews, and Christians lived side by side, practising their own religion and engaging in their own artistic pursuits. Of course, this does not mean that there was no interchange of ideas between the different groups. Obviously, Spanish craftsmen sometimes worked on Mudejar works of art, and Mohammedans, on the other hand, executed designs in the Western style. In addition to this, the Christian rulers often encouraged expressions of the Eastern spirit in their territories.

In 1502 the Moorish subjects of Castile and León were obliged to emigrate or turn Christian. This law was extended to Aragon in 1526, but did not result in any profound artistic change. Instead of petering out, with the arrival of the modern age, Mudejar art began to cultivate its popular appeal so that by the second quarter of the sixteenth century there was a clear difference between the art of the court, already turning to Italian models, and popular art with its roots in Mudejarism, which thus maintained an independent existence until well into the seventeenth century. The publication of treatises like that on carpentry by Diego López de Arenas, which appeared in 1633, helped to perpetuate Islamic techniques and characteristics, in particular a vein of anticlassicism which was to become an important part of the Spanish heritage.

The Mudejar style is distinguished by the use of Islamic elements, like the horseshoe arch, by a marked tendency toward ornament, based on geometrical motifs, and by a preference for using bricks in building.

Architecture

The history of Mudejar architecture dates from the second half of the twelfth century, when Mudejar structures began to appear next to or in place of those of the Romanesque. The earliest architectural expressions of Mudejar art are to be found in the cloister of San Juan de Duero, in Soria, with its different types of arcade, and in the domes of the cathedrals of Zamora, Toro, and Salamanca. The latter was under construction in 1163 or 1164.

Although the more primitive examples have not survived, it appears evident that the capital of Mudejar art in Castile was Toledo. The Mudejar part of the mosque, which had been converted into the church of Cristo de la Luz, was built about 1187. The consecration of the church of San Román in 1221 was soon followed by the building of the church of Santiago del Arrabal. Its towers, like that of Santo Tomé, served as prototypes.

Another important Mudejar center was the region between Avila and León. In Sahagún (León) there are two exceptionally interesting churches, San Tirso and San Lorenzo, with blind arcades in the apses and large belfries, all constructed in brick. Some of the chapels built under Christian rule in cities with longstanding Moorish traditions are more conspicuously Islamic. Such is the case with the Royal Chapel in the Mosque of Cordova built between 1258 and 1260 by order of Alfonso X. Its carved plaster panels continue the great tradition, though the Nasrid element is evident in the tiled socles, striking lion brackets, and plaster cornices.

Later, in the second half of the thirteenth century, it became common to find Gothic and Mudejar construction existing side by side.

It was in Aragon, however, that Mudejar Gothic flourished best. The most ancient examples of the style are certain remains, dating from about 1200, in various of the churches of Daroca. The increase in building activity in the fourteenth century led to the construction of numerous churches with bell towers, often free-standing. The most important examples are doubtless the towers of the churches. They are of three types: square, octagonal, and mixed, that is with a transition from a square to an eight-sided plan. Their relative antiquity can be judged from the fact that the older towers are generally simpler and

102 (Left) Façade of the Alcázar of Seville. Fourteenth century.

103 (Right) Detail of the interior, synagogue of El Tránsito, Toledo. c. 1355

often superior in style. The beautiful octagonal tower of Santa Maria de Tauste (Saragossa) dates from the middle of the thirteenth century; that of the Cathedral of Teruel was begun in 1259. The latter has a square plan and coupled windows and ends in an octagonal belfry with a lantern. The square towers of the churches of El Salvador (Plate 100) and San Martín, both in Teruel, date from the fourteenth century; the treatment of the brick surfaces suggests the appearance of an embroidered carpet. The mixed style is represented by the tower of the church of Utebo (Saragossa), built at a somewhat later date. The relation of all these structures to the oriental minaret is best exemplified in the tower of San Andrés de Calatayud (Saragossa).

During the thirteenth century and the centuries that followed, numerous Mudejar churches, chapels, and monasteries were built south of Toledo and all the way to the Portuguese frontier. In many

104   Castle of Coca (Seville). Fifteenth century

instances, the most interesting part of the structure is the dome, which is generally highly ornamental. The monastery of Guadalupe (Cáceres) has a cloister and chapel, dating from about 1390, wholly in the Islamic style.

The architects of the palaces built for kings and nobles were even more ready to employ Mudejar forms. The refinement achieved by the Spanish Mohammedans became something of an obsession with the Christians. Thus, between 1340 and 1344, Alfonso XI built a magnificent palace on Moorish lines at Tordesillas on the banks of the Douro (Plate 101). The most important Mudejar palace to survive, however, is the Alcázar of Seville, built by Pedro I during the last third of the fourteenth century (Plate 102). In its construction Pedro made use of part of an existing Almohade structure and brought in craftsmen provided by his friend, the Nasrid monarch Mohammed V, as well as workmen from Toledo and Seville. Striking elements of the palace, progressively enriched during the fifteenth century, are the façade and the Hall of the Ambassadors. Inscriptions reveal that these date from 1362 and 1366 respectively. The style has much in common with that of Granada. Other important features of the Alcázar are the Patio de las Doncellas and the Patio de las Muñecas, the former with cusped pointed arches, and both decorated with elaborate, though repetitive, quasi-abstract motifs.

Numerous Mudejar palaces, dating from the fourteenth, fifteenth, and sixteenth centuries, are also to be found in other Spanish cities. Prominent among them are the convent of Santa Maria la Real in Toledo, founded in 1477, and the remains of the Casa de los Caballeros de Santiago in Cordova. In these buildings the taste for ornament becomes progressively more marked and, during the second half of the fifteenth century, merged first with Burgundian and Flemish, and then with Italian influences, all within the framework of the Plateresque style. This complicated synthesis, which might appear strange were it not so thoroughly in keeping with the general Spanish experience, produced some very important architecture, to which we shall return later. At this point, however, we should at least mention the sixteenth-century Casa de Pilato (Pilate's House) in Seville, for the sake of the purity of its Islamic style.

Among the more important Mudejar buildings erected in Spain during the later Middle Ages are the synagogues; lacking a style of their own, they adopted the congenial forms and techniques of the Moors. There is a notable synagogue in Cordova, built by Isaac Mejeb in about 1314, but the finest of these structures is the famous synagogue of the Tránsito in Toledo, built by the taxgatherer of King Pedro I, Samuel ha-Levi, between 1355 and 1357 (Plate 103). Its spatial simplicity is in striking contrast with the magnificence of the carved stucco and the intricate collar-beam and rafter framing of the roof. The stucco reliefs in these buildings are some of the best in the whole of Spanish art, combining lacy fretwork with floral motifs that clearly betray Gothic influence. The Mudejar style was also applied to certain structures of a civil character such as bridges, hospitals, and baths, like those at Gerona.

Finally, we should not omit to mention the Mudejar influence on military architecture, which finds expression not only in the use of brick but also in a certain ornamentalism and the persistence of Islamic elements, such as the horseshoe arch and the breastwork. Among the more important of these military structures are the Puerta del Sol, forming part of the walls of Toledo, the front of which is pierced by archways in the Granadan style, the Gate of Cantalapiedra in Madrigal de las Altas Torres, and the formidable castles of La Mota, in Medina del Campo (Valladolid), Coca (Segovia), and Arévalo (Avila). The most typically Mudejar of these is the castle of Coca, the brick walls of which appear once to have been in polychrome, their smoothness contrasting with the severe geometry of the clustered turrets (Plate 104).

The Applied Arts

A novel aspect of Mudejar architecture was the application of decoration to the exterior as well as the interior of buildings. The decorative arts experienced a vigorous development, particularly from the quantitative point of view, since economic progress had brought within the reach of the knights and bourgeoisie many luxury items, once available only to royalty and the upper nobility.

Mudejar art is many-sided, but in general may be regarded as an extension of Nasrid art with certain Gothic overtones. Mudejar carpentry and cabinetmaking are particularly noteworthy, both for the sumptuousness of carved and painted wainscots and ceilings and for the greater severity of doors wrought with geometrical motifs. Some particularly fine wainscoting is found in the chapter house of the monastery of Sijena, in Santo Domingo de Silos and Santa Maria de Maluenda in Saragossa. The magnificent ceiling of the great nave of Teruel cathedral, with paintings revealing a distinctly Gothic influence, dates from the end of the thirteenth century. A much later example, in which the Mudejar style is allied with that of the Renaissance, is the ceiling of the throne room in the Aljafería of Saragossa. The Mudejar carpenters also built wooden domes like that of the Hall of the Ambassadors in the Alcázar of Seville, made by Master Diego Ruiz in 1427.

Elegantly carved stuccoes, porcelain plaques, and decorative paintings were turned out in profusion by Mudejar craftsmen. Among the original techniques they employed were graffito and the art of making mocarabes in stone. An exceptional example of the novel use of ceramics in architectural decoration is the dome of the Chapel of San Gregorio of the Concepción Francisca of Toledo, dating from 1422.

Mudejar potters produced pieces of great beauty in Teruel, Paterna (Plate 106), and Manises. The decoration is inexhaustibly varied and imaginative, a common procedure being to stamp fine motifs in the wet clay, finishing off the design with stylized floral patterns pricked in with a punch. The lusterware of the Valencian potteries, which by 1400 were beginning to achieve a clear superiority over those of Málaga, is distinguished by its greater refinement and wealth of forms and ornament. Blue and "gold" predominate in the decoration of these pieces, which, by 1450, turned mainly on heraldic motifs, sometimes with the inclusion of Gothic letters.

The supremacy of Mudejar cabinetmaking is revealed by the fact that between the thirteenth and fifteenth century most Spanish religious furniture was made in that style. An excellent example, showing carved plasterwork ornamentation, is afforded by a set of choir stalls from Gradefes (León). Sumptuous artistry, influenced by the Gothic, distinguishes such pieces as the triptych from the monastery of Piedra (Saragossa), now in the Royal Academy of History, Madrid (Plate 105), and the cupboard from Toledo known as the Templars' Pharmacy (Victoria and Albert Museum, London). In general, Mudejar influence is discernible in the carved decoration of Spanish furniture until the seventeenth century, and, more faintly, even much later.

Among the products of the metalworkers, which included gates, weapons, lamps, candlesticks, censers, and so forth, we might single out the fifteenth-century silvergilt casket of the abbey of Roncesvalles (Navarre). Many of the Spanish techniques of working silver, copper, and brass are of Mudejar origin, like those employed by the famous swordsmiths of Toledo, Cuenca, and other centers.

Though textiles are not as well represented as the products of the other minor arts, enough have been preserved to enable us to reconstruct the development of textile technology and ornament. Silks, painted fabrics, tapestries, braid, and such, amply demonstrate the skill of the Mudejar weavers. Among the more important finds are various pieces from the tomb of Don Fernando de la Cerda (died 1275), in the monastery of Las Huelgas at Burgos, and the cope of the Toledan Archbishop Don Sancho (1266–1275), bearing the arms of León and Castile. Carpets of Islamic design were produced in the workshops of Christian Spain from the fourteenth to the seventeenth century. The most ancient fall into two groups: those called Almirante, in dark, stern colors, dominated by blues, somber reds, and deep browns; and those, gayer and brighter in tone, said to be of the Holbein type, because Hans Holbein included such a carpet in one of his paintings. Leather was employed for a variety of artistic purposes, the leatherworkers being skilled in a host of techniques, including tooling, engraving, *repoussé*, embossing, and the application of gilt and color.

106   Paterna dish. Fourteenth century. Museum of Ancient Art, Barcelona.

Chapter V

The Renaissance

During the fifteenth century, Spanish manifestations of the Renaissance spirit were few and scattered. The encroachments of humanist culture, profane art, and the prestige of classical antiquity were at first merely sporadic. Wrapped in medieval tradition and strongly influenced by the Mudejar contribution to its art, Spain did not find it easy to accept the new philosophy and aesthetics that swept triumphantly across the frontiers of Italy into the rest of Europe.

Certain factors, however, were working in favor of a new concept of the nature of life and art. One was the political and economic situation during the reigns of Ferdinand of Aragon and Isabella of Castile; another the national optimism released by final victory over the Moors and the discovery of America; a third the transformation of the medieval castle into a palace. Don Iñigo López de Mendoza, the second count of Tendilla, did much to introduce the new style. On his return from Italy, where he had been sent to make peace between Rome and Naples, he brought with him a number of prominent Italian intellectuals and artists, including Lucio Marineo of Sicily, Baldassare Castiglione, Antonio Geraldino, and others. Cardinal Cisneros encouraged the assimilation of Renaissance ideas by establishing an important study center in Alcalá de Henares.

PLATERESQUE ARCHITECTURE

In architecture, the distinguishing features of the Renaissance style are, above all, the substitution of the rounded arch for the pointed arch of the Gothic, grotesque decoration, and the use of Greco-Roman columns and pilasters.

The earliest examples may be regarded as transitional: buildings combining a Gothic structure with classical decoration, or vice versa. At the same time, in a reversal of the usual pattern, architecture tended to fall under the influence of the minor arts, with their refined techniques and lively spirit of invention. Finally, certain persistent and distinctly Spanish characteristics grafted themselves upon the new forms.

In this way there arose the Plateresque style: influenced by carpentry, by Mudejar art, and by the unrestrained ornamentalism of the Isabella of Castile style, though indebted for its repertory of forms to Italian and classical sources. The term Plateresque comes from the Spanish word *platero*, silversmith. This style appealed to something deeply rooted in the Spanish temperament, love of the façade, that is, a surface covered with decorative and allegorical elements. It persisted for more than half a century, gradually giving way to a sterner, more formalistic manner that leaned more toward a strictly geometrical distribution of the masses.

Lorenzo Vázquez, the Mendozas' architect, was one of the pioneers of the Plateresque. His share in the Colegio de Santa Cruz in Valladolid suggests that he was also the author of the superb palace of Cogolludo and the Mendoza palace, both in Guadalajara, buildings of the early sixteenth century that define the ultimate direction to be taken by the new style. Vázquez was followed by Enrique de Egas, architect of the ostentatious Hospital of the Holy Cross in Toledo, begun in 1504. Although many traces of Gothic influence still remain, the ornament is thoroughly Renaissance in character. Pediments, friezes of grotesques, reliefs, scalloped backgrounds, and escutcheons, separated by classical pilasters, are typical of the decoration. The monumental stairway, approached through a trio of noble arches, is particularly impressive (Plate 107). The Mudejar spirit is manifested not so much in the forms as in the insistent rhythms of the decorated surfaces. Before the building was completed, another architect intervened. He was Alonso Covarrubias, whose youthful design for the monumental altar and tomb of Santa Librada in Sigüenza cathedral, executed between 1515 and 1518, presages the extraordinary quality of the works of his maturity.

During the first half of the sixteenth century, a series of important buildings were erected in Castile, linked by a common style that radiated from the city of Toledo. One of these is the hall of the university in Alcalá de Henares, with stuccoes in the "Cisneros style," a term referring to the period of that cardinal's regency. In Toledo cathedral, the magnificent antechamber of the chapter house, with its mixture of Plateresque and Mudejar elements, dates from the years 1504–1512. More advanced in design is the Chapel of the New Kings, built by Covarrubias, who laid his proposals before the court in 1531. The doorway of St. John's Chapel in the same cathedral includes certain elements of undeniably Gothic ancestry handled in a new and wholly Renaissance spirit.

In Burgos, the Renaissance slowly acquired distinctive local char-

acteristics, starting with work which the presence of an inner Gothicism stamps as Plateresque. The most important examples are to be found in the cathedral: the door of La Pellejería, built by Francisco de Colonia, which includes some purely Italian details, and the profusely decorated monumental dome by Juan de Vallejo. Other noteworthy buildings erected in the Burgos area during the same period include the palace of Miranda in Peñaranda de Duero, with a large porticoed patio and a broad façade in which Mudejar and Plateresque elements are combined with traces of Gothic.

The greatest achievements of the Burgos Plateresque, however, we owe to Diego de Siloé, son of the Master Gil de Siloé, author of so much of the fine Gothic sculpture in the Carthusian monastery of Miraflores. Diego de Siloé is mentioned for the first time in 1517,

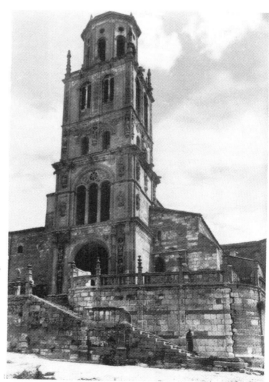

107 (Left) Enrique de Egas. Stairway, Hospital of the Holy Cross, Toledo. c. 1520

108 (Right) Diego de Siloé. Tower of Santa Maria del Campo (Burgos). c. 1527

when he was in Naples working in collaboration with Bartolomé Ordóñez. Four years later he executed in the so-called Golden Staircase (in the Cathedral of Burgos), one of the most beautiful creations in Plateresque art. One of Siloé's architectural projects, designed in 1527, is the elegant tower of Santa Maria del Campo, a prismatic structure divided into a succession of zones, a drastic departure from tradition (Plate 108).

Siloé was one of the great figures of the Spanish Renaissance. Since his subsequent work in Granada is marked by a radical change in style, it will be discussed in a later chapter.

Plateresque architecture is at its most original in Salamanca. The Casa de las Conchas reflects the stylistic influence of the circle of Lorenzo Vázquez. Though late Gothic in conception, the New Cathedral of Salamanca, founded in 1513, is infiltrated with Plateresque ornament (Plate 109). Similarly, the famous façade of the university has its Gothic elements, particularly noticeable in the construction of the two segmental arches and the cresting, though in general it is much more advanced and Plateresque. Grotesque figures, angels and demons, putti, escutcheons, fantastic animals, and military trophies bubble all over this admirable façade, but its chief characteristics are the subordination of details to the overall effect and to the even level of the surface, which points to the generic relationship between the Plateresque and the art of the goldsmith (Plate 111).

One of the most talented architects to adopt the Plateresque style was Rodrigo Gil de Hontañón, whose career ran from 1523 to 1577. Son of Master Juan, who worked with Simon of Cologne in Burgos, his name appears for the first time, alongside that of his father, in connection with the building of the New Cathedral of Salamanca. Also in Salamanca, he later built a number of palaces of interest, like the richly ornamented palace of the Count of Monterrey, designed in 1539, and the Palace of Fonseca. In these buildings there is still something reminiscent of the Gothic and Mudejar styles. Rodrigo's masterpiece, the University of Alcalá de Henares (1541–1553), however, not only appears free of these traces of the past, but represents a definite

109   Interior of the New Cathedral of Salamanca.

forward step in the history of the Spanish Plateresque. Its façade, in particular, is one of the most harmonious ever built in this style (Plate 110). A remarkable refinement of execution goes hand in hand with the superior quality of the design. A few carvings, lightly contrasted, enrich the central zone of the building at the main and upper levels. The ensemble, though ruled by the strictest symmetry, leaves an impression of spirited elegance.

Southern Spain possesses a valuable group of Plateresque buildings, both civil and religious. The most significant of these is undoubtedly the Cathedral of Plasencia. In 1497 the director of works was the Toledan Enrique de Egas, who continued in this position until work was suspended in 1513. Eight years later it was resumed by Juan de Alava, who was later succeeded by Covarrubias and Siloé. In this building the most important Plateresque feature is the main front, the work of Juan de Alava. Alava divided the surface into four horizontal zones which he balanced with the vertical rhythms of two groups of three columns, one on either side of the porch. The Renaissance reached Andalusia by way of the Castilian schools. In civil and religious architecture Gothicism gave way to classical forms, though not without producing the usual hybrids. One important building, the town hall of Seville, has a perfectly classical façade, begun in 1527. Andalusian Plateresque is exemplified by the collegiate church of Osuna, built between 1534 and 1539, and Cordova cathedral, begun in 1523 and completed in 1607. By an unfortunate error of judgment, the latter was erected in the middle of the great Mosque of Cordova, part of which had to be demolished for the purpose. Doorways and courts of many Andalusian palaces testify to the skill of the carvers, who decorated them with Mudejar motifs: the Merchants' Exchange in Granada, and the Casa de las Dueñas in Seville, are worthy of mention. Most of the architects remained faithful to the traditional building materials of Andalusia: brick, carved stucco, glazed tile, and wood.

The Plateresque style was eventually carried to the north of Spain, where, in Galicia, it appears in a number of fine buildings, such as the Hospital in Santiago de Compostela and the church of Santa Maria la grande in Pontevedra. One of the more significant buildings of the second quarter of the sixteenth century is the convent of San Marcos in León.

Its typically Spanish façade is richly decorated with reliefs, mostly executed between 1533 and 1541, one of the chief carvers being Juan de Badajoz. Among the other craftsmen in the area were the brothers Jerónimo and Juan Corral, authors of the magnificent chapel of the Benavente in the church of Santa Maria at Medina de Rioseco (1544–1546), and of the so-called Casa Blanca, completed in 1563, in Medina del Campo.

The Basque provinces and Navarre possess few noteworthy examples of the Plateresque, which was occasionally employed for civil architecture and certain secondary religious structures. Nevertheless, we should at least mention the University of Oñate. Its original pilasters with sculptured corners were commissioned from the Frenchman Picart in 1545.

At the beginning of the sixteenth century, building activity in Aragón was at a high point. In general, Aragonese architecture is characterized by the use of regional materials, mainly in the Mudejar tradition (brick, stucco, woodwork). The porch of the convent of Santa Engracia in Saragossa, begun about 1512, is an important example of the pure Plateresque. Carved by the elder Gil Morlanes, it was conceived as a retable façade. Brick was used for the palace of the Audiencia in Saragossa, a large and nobly proportioned structure, begun in 1551. In Calayatud, the porch of the church of Santa Maria is a fine example of Aragonese Plateresque.

Diego de Siloé and Alonso de Covarrubias are the two architects chiefly responsible for the decisive advance from the essentially decorative architecture of the Plateresque to the classical canon of the pure Renaissance. The former was summoned to Granada in 1528 to supervise the construction of the cathedral, begun five years before. In 1537, the great artist completed the apse and the transept, where his genius is proclaimed both by the grandeur of the Roman triumphal arches and by the beauty of the ornamental reliefs. Siloé's powers are best displayed in the central chapel, a circular area more than 130 feet high and 65 feet wide. Its principal elements include Corinthian columns, a vigorous entablature with a carved frieze, and three tiers of windows with round arches that impose their rhythm on the space, while at the same time flooding it with light. During the first period of his stay in Granada, Siloé designed the magnificent Colegio de

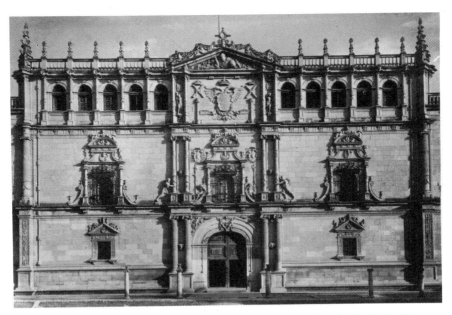

Santiago in Salamanca, one of the most refined accomplishments of the Plateresque.

Covarrubias' stylistic transformation evidently resulted in the construction of the splendid Alcazar of Toledo, begun in 1545. This castle-palace, with its rectangular plan, four tall corner towers, and imposing walls rhythmically pierced with windows, served as a model for other Spanish structures of the same type. From Toledo the new style was carried to Cuenca, where, in the second third of the sixteenth century, the cathedral was enriched with additional decorations, in particular, a very beautiful arch by Jamete, a French sculptor who came to Spain in 1535, working in Toledo under Covarrubias before undertaking the Cuencan project.

At this point we should mention another important work: the

additions to Murcia cathedral by an Italian artist, Jacobo Florentín, called "El Indaco." During the second quarter of the sixteenth century, Florentín continued the work on the cathedral tower and completed the decoration of the magnificent doors of the sacristy, blending the sculpture into the fabric of the structure with extraordinary sureness and vigor.

Prominent among the Andalusian religious buildings of this period are the cathedrals of Málaga, Jaén, and Guadix, and the church of San Salvador in Ubeda, which we owe to another fine artist, Andrés de Vandelvira, who combines a certain subtle Mannerism with formulas inherited from Florentín and Siloé. The Hospital of St. James in Ubeda is from Vandelvira's final period and marks the transition to the sterner style of the last third of the sixteenth century.

THE CLASSICAL PERIOD

Perhaps the finest piece of Renaissance architecture in Spain is the palace of Charles V in Granada. This is a work of more than national importance, not only for its exceptional quality, but also because it is one of the very few existing Renaissance buildings with a circular court. It was built by Pedro Machuca, architect, sculptor, and painter, born in Toledo, who studied in Italy with Michelangelo. This must have been sometime before 1520, since we know that in that year he was back in Spain. In 1526, shortly after their marriage, Charles V and Isabella of Portugal stayed for a while in the Alhambra, and it was during this visit that the emperor decided to build a royal palace in the area. Work began one year later.

Machuca, who doubtless was well acquainted with the classical Italian monuments, developed a style remarkable for its intensity and harmony. He divided the palace into two zones, sharply separated by a cornice. The general decoration does not consist of sculptured reliefs, but derives from the contrast between the structural elements of the design. The rough-cut stone blocks of the lower zone, similar to that of Florentine palaces, sustain the calmer surface of the zone above, punctuated by pilasters and windows. The porches are further emphasized by the use of gray marble rather than the reddish sandstone

208

employed for the rest of the building. Medallions with escutcheons and allegorical reliefs constitute its sober ornamentation. The interior court, with its two tiers of columns and animated circular rhythms, has a character of its own, lighter than that of the façades (Plate 112).

The Escorial

In the great monastery of the Escorial we are confronted with a concept different from that which normally prevails in the architecture of the Spanish Renaissance. The extreme sobriety of the ornament and the total predominance of the structural elements, its grandeur, its geometrical austerity, rightly compared with that of the Pyramids, and the simplicity of its contours, graceful, certainly, bring us closer to its true nature. This is unrelated or rather runs contrary to the mainstream of Mudejar and vital popular art, but it is equally, if not more Spanish, and, in fact, has become a paradigm of Spanish ambition in the Golden Century. The truth is that this enormous building better represented the spirit of a resolute age, and that of the monarch who ordered its construction, watched over the details, and chose his workers with such care.

Philip II built the Escorial in fulfillment of a vow made during the siege of Saint-Quentin, which he finally captured in August, 1557. The cold, rationalistic temperament of the monarch and his tendency to theocracy will forever be identified with this work. Philip also knew how to choose the interpreters of his thought, for, ignoring the more prominent architects of his reign, he fixed upon a complete unknown, the Italian-trained Juan Bautista de Toledo.

The general plan of the monastery was prepared in 1559. It is an almost square structure, with bare walls and corner towers, enclosing seventeen courts and, in the center, a church (Plate 113). On his death in 1567, Juan Bautista de Toledo was succeeded by Juan de Herrera, who had the satisfaction of witnessing the completion of the dome of the church in 1582. Juan Bautista de Toledo had been able to build the admirable Patio de los Evangelistas, the great south front, and certain of the towers. Later, Herrera partially modified the designs of his predecessor, leaving the church in the dominant position it occupied in the original plan, but reflecting it in the west wall by

means of a crowning element rising above the façade. Like the geometry of the corner towers, its detail accentuates the bareness of the enormous walls on either side.

Through this western façade one enters the Patio de los Reyes, a great court in the Vitruvian manner, leading to the doors of the church. The arrangement of this church is copied from certain obvious models, in particular St. Peter's in Rome, though the differences in form and spirit are more important than the affinities. In the Escorial an impression of continuous, solid stonework imposes itself upon the airy articulation of the masses. The presbytery contains the royal tombs of Charles I and Philip II, with bronze statues by the Leoni. Inside the

112   (Facing) Pedro Machuca. Court of the Palace of Charles V. Granada. c. 1530

113   Juan Bautista de Toledo and Juan de Herrera. The Escorial (Madrid). 1559–1582

church, where the general severity of the architecture is most profoundly felt, the Doric order prevails, the effect of grandeur reaching a climax beneath the dome. The qualities of marble, stone, and bronze are combined in compact forms. The cornices and the fine fluting of the pilasters stand out amid this purely geometrical beauty.

The 656-foot-long walls of the monastery have lead to its being described as a "horizontal skyscraper," but the impression that prevails throughout the Escorial is by no means one of merely material and utilitarian grandeur.

SIXTEENTH-CENTURY SCULPTURE

In Spain the transition to the sculpture of the Renaissance did not signify a general change of theme: the traditional religious iconography and certain essentials of the Gothic were firmly retained. At the same time, the Renaissance style is characterized by greater freedom and naturalism, and, within its limits, by great variety. Early in the sixteenth century, numerous artists of diverse origin—Flemings, Frenchmen, Italians—came and settled in the Iberian Peninsula. These men helped to instill the Renaissance spirit, but they were also responsible for its eclecticism and multiformity. At first, a great deal was imported from abroad, later, the output of immigrant and native artists became sufficient to satisfy the demand.

The Frenchman Philip Vigarny, did much to establish the Renaissance style in Burgos, where he arrived in 1498. The distinguishing characteristics of his work, both as a sculptor and as an architect, are love of order and correctness of form. In his reliefs, which reveal a

114   Bartolomé Ordóñez. Tomb of Don Felipe and Doña Juana. c.1519. Marble. Royal Chapel of Granada

Overleaf 115 and 116:

(Left) Vasco de la Zarza. Detail of the tomb of Don Alonso de Madrigal. 1518. Marble. Cathedral of Avila. (Right) Damián Forment. Detail of the retable of the high altar of the Cathedral of Huesca. 1520–1534. Marble

most painstaking narrative technique, he employs the pictorial devices of perspective to suggest distance and the various zones of space. The year he arrived in Burgos he was commissioned to carve the alabaster reliefs in the ambulatory of the cathedral. The finest of these Gospel scenes is the Road to Calvary, which achieves eloquence without descending into rhetoric. Vigarny was also the author of four of the scenes that constitute the great retable of Toledo cathedral, and in 1505 he was entrusted with the retable of Palencia cathedral. He also carved the reliefs of the choir stalls in the cathedrals of Burgos and Toledo, those in Toledo dating from 1535. Sometimes Vigarny collaborated with Diego de Siloé, and sometimes with Alonso Berruguete; his style is recognizable as the more restrained, naturalistic, and more purely Renaissance of the three.

In 1519, Diego de Siloé, whose work as an architect we have already discussed, after completing the Golden Staircase in the Cathedral of Burgos between 1519 and 1523, carved the retable of the Condestable's Chapel in collaboration with Vigarny. Siloé's style is characterized by a pathos best expressed in the superb Christ at Burgos, and the Ecce Homo of San Agustín de Dueñas. In 1525 he started work on the choir stalls of San Benito in Valladolid. His influence was as great in Andalusia as in Castile.

Although born in Burgos, Bartolomé Ordóñez worked first in Italy. In 1515 he was in Barcelona working on the choir of the cathedral. His well-composed reliefs and splendid marble panels, so severely monumental and harmonious, suggest the influence of Michelangelo. In about 1519 he must have executed the admirable tomb of Don Felipe and Doña Juana in the Royal Chapel of Granada (Plate 114). A year later he died in Carrara, leaving behind him numerous admirers and imitators of his pure and noble style.

In the second decade of the sixteenth century, the Renaissance travelled from Burgos to Palencia. During this period, however, Palencian sculpture is chiefly oriented toward Juan de Valmaseda, who was still strongly attached to the Gothic tradition. Valmaseda was born about 1490; the first references to his activities mention his presence in Burgos, though he doubtless worked in various other cities, vitalizing them with his original style. In 1519 he carved the Calvary of the retable of Palencia cathedral, where the pathos is idealized by a great capacity for creating beauty. Valmaseda worked on a number of important monuments, the finest of which is the retable of St. Alphonsus in the same cathedral.

During the sixteenth century, immense retables continued to be erected in the churches and cathedrals of Spain. The fabric of the retable, based on superposed orders and rich ornament, became almost as important as the numerous statues and narrative reliefs. When the retable was carved in stone or marble, the influence of carpentry determined its form.

During the sixteenth century, the principal center of the art in New Castile was the city of Toledo. Gothic forms persisted there, but the Renaissance style reached the area prematurely. The sculptor whose work prepared its entry was Vasco de la Zarza, who remained active there until his death in 1524. Zarza may have been trained in Italy or under Fancelli in Avila. The affinity between his style and that of the Italian sculptor is revealed in the magnificent tomb in Toledo cathedral carved for his protector, Don Juan Carrillo de Albornoz, in which the delicate Plateresque ornamentation is combined with a classical outline. In 1518 he completed his most famous work: the ostentatious tomb of Don Alonso de Madrigal, behind the high altar in Avila cathedral (Plate 115). Far from submerging the figure of Don Alonso, the wealth of decoration glitters around him like an allegory of the treasures of the spiritual and religious life. The style of Vasco de la Zarza exerted a broad influence in Toledo, Avila, and Segovia.

In Andalusia, the spirit of Mercadante of Brittany still persisted. Among the masters who introduced the Renaissance was Jorge Fernández, the author of various sculptures in the portal of the Royal Chapel of Granada, carved about 1517 and still steeped in Gothicism. Castilian influence first made itself felt in the design of the choir stalls of Jaén cathedral, becoming more firmly established with the arrival of Diego de Siloé, to whom we owe the extremely beautiful reliefs of the choir stalls of San Jerónimo in Granada, and the praying statues of the Catholic Kings in the Royal Chapel of the same city.

In Aragon, the Renaissance arrived prematurely with the sculptor Gil Morlanes the Elder, who in 1506 completed the alabaster retable of the monastery of Montearagón (Huesca cathedral). Sumptuous

117 Juan de Juni. The Entombment. c.1550. Polychrome wood. National Museum of Religious Carvings, Valladolid

118 (Facing) Alonso Berruguete. The Annunciation. In the retable from La Mejorada, Olmedo (Valladolid). c.1525. Polychrome wood. National Museum of Religious Carvings, Valladolid

Overleaf 119 and 120:

(Left) Pedro de Campaña. The Descent from the Cross. 1547. Cathedral of Seville. (Right) Luis de Morales. Ecce Homo. Hispanic Society of America, New York

218

retables in stone and alabaster are more common than those in wood. The most significant sculptor of the sixteenth century was Damián Forment, who is known to have worked in Valencia shortly after the year 1500. In 1509 he set up his workshop in Saragossa, where he remained until his death in 1540, without ceasing to maintain his contacts with the Mediterranean coast. His art is dominated by a severe decorative concept that lends variety to the composition without degenerating into restlessness. In 1509 he undertook to carve the superb retable of Nuestra Señora del Pilar in Saragossa, a work in a mixed style, with Renaissance figures surrounded by Gothic ornament. We are indebted to Forment for the retable of Huesca cathedral, completed in 1534 (Plate 116). His original design for the great retable of the monastery of Poblet, commissioned in 1527, is also one of his masterpieces. During the sixteenth century, Forment's style played an important part in the development of Spanish sculpture, producing a number of notable sculptors.

The second third of the sixteenth century witnessed the culmination of Spanish Renaissance sculpture. Once the various foreign elements had been unified and integrated with the national character, an expressive power, derived in part from religious ideals, surged into the Renaissance forms, turning them to its own ends. The foreign masters who came to Spain no longer dictated their own style, but acted as interpreters of the spirit to which they were exposed. This period was presided over by a sculptor of genius: Alonso Berruguete, son of the painter Pedro Berruguete, born about 1488 in Paredes de Nava. In about 1508 he went to Italy and studied under Michelangelo. In 1517 he was back in Valladolid. His art is spread over a number of cities: Saragossa, Granada, Toledo, and Medina del Campo. Though the source of his style lies in the Florentine Renaissance, its essential originality appears to be derived from the personality of the sculptor himself.

Berruguete enlarged the conventional range of figures, distorting them, both to achieve pictorial effects and to heighten the pathos. He used polychromy, taking advantage of the reflections from gold to surround his figures with an air of unrest. His first important work to be recorded is the retable of the Mejorada (1525), now in the Valladolid Museum (Plate 118). In 1526 he was commissioned to carve the retable of San Benito de Valladolid, since dismantled but still preserved in the museum of that city. The figures of saints that form part of this altarpiece are among the most expressive he ever produced. In 1541 he must have executed the superb choir-stall reliefs in Toledo cathedral, a commission he shared with Vigarny. Here the figures are impetuous and tormented, but always under the control of an inspiration certain of its own resources. Berruguete also carved the episcopal throne, which is topped by an admirable Transfiguration; one panel, showing the Crossing of the Red Sea, is notable for its linear rhythm of the utmost originality. In 1554, Berruguete was commissioned to carve the tomb of Cardinal Tavera, which was finished shortly before the artist's death.

One of the more interesting of the foreign artists who worked in Spain during the second third of the sixteenth century is the Frenchman Juan de Juni, whose sculpture is noted for its spirituality, manifested in full and beautiful forms, natural in their proportions but declamatory in their distortion of gesture. Juni may have been trained in Italy, since his art shows evidence of contact with the Lombard Renaissance and Michelangelo. In about 1533 he appears in León, but by 1541 he was settled in Valladolid. Several of his works deserve individual mention, among them the retables in Valladolid and Burgo de Osma cathedrals, and the Entombment in Segovia cathedral, dating from 1571, which combines figures on the same theme forming part of another Entombment, preserved in the Museum in Valladolid (Plate 117).

The sculptors of the last third of the sixteenth century worked under the influence of the great personalities of the preceding epoch, upon whose characteristics they superimposed certain Mannerist tendencies, with signs of a transition to the Baroque. The most important was Juan de Anchieta, born in Azpeitia (Guipúzcoa) in about 1540. In 1565 he was in Valladolid, but in about 1578 he moved to Pamplona, where he lived until his death in 1588. Anchieta's most conspicuous quality is grandeur of form, which developed into a virtual obsession with the heroic and the monumental. His influence spread throughout the area in which he worked, thanks, in part, to the efforts of his collaborators and disciples.

During this period, the religious art we have briefly described was

223

paralleled by a sculpture inspired by the court and closely associated with the ambitious projects of Charles I and Philip II, particularly the Escorial. The principal sculptors of this group were the Italians León and Pompeo Leoni, born in Arezzo and established in Milan, before they transferred their activities to Spain. Their style is a synthesis of Mannerism and Academicism, intended primarily to exalt their subjects. The most important sculptures of León and Pompeyo Leoni are the bronze effigies of the Empress Isabella and Philip II in the Prado Museum, and the groups forming part of the mausoleums of Charles V and Philip II in the Escorial. Theirs is a hieratic and sumptuous art, reflecting the glory of an empire at the time of its supremacy.

SIXTEENTH-CENTURY PAINTING

In Spain, as in other European countries, sixteenth-century painting is characterized by eclecticism, or rather by the synthesis of a number of different trends: national tendencies, the influence of the great Italian masters, and certain elements of the art of Northern and Central Europe. In the early years of the century, the formula was thoroughly *Quattrocento,* but the use of oils and a growing interest in naturalistic representation and the manipulation of space nullified or progressively diluted the surviving Gothic characteristics. With the passage of time gold backgrounds became increasingly rare, and landscapes gained in breadth and luminosity. Many Spanish artists visited Italy, attracted by the fame of the Italian schools. While there, some underwent a technical and aesthetic transformation, and, on returning to Spain, contributed decisively to the growth of the Renaissance spirit, spreading their version of the great lessons to be learned from the art of Leonardo, Raphael, and Michelangelo. These influences remained dominant until the middle of the century, though, as we have mentioned, not without interference from Flanders, Germany, and Holland.

The most important characteristic distinguishing the Renaissance painting of Spain from that of Italy, France, and Germany relates more to subject matter than to style. It is the Spanish rejection of mythological themes and the cult of the nude. The Spanish artist of the sixteenth century shared the spirituality of his Gothic forebears; in general, he worked for the churches and monasteries, or for nobles with similar religious preoccupations. Many of the better paintings of this period are imbued with the mysticism of the ascetic, and are remote not only from the sensualism associated with paganistic themes, but also from the cult of art for art's sake and sheer aestheticism. The foreigners who came to work in Spain during this period, which, it must be remembered, coincided with the peak of Spanish imperial power, were quickly assimilated. Far from resisting the established tradition in Spain, they sometimes became among its most passionate interpreters.

The Influence of Leonardo

Spanish painting was given a new and more determined thrust in the direction of the Renaissance by two artists trained in Italy: Fernando Yáñez de la Almedina and Fernando Llanos. In 1507 they were jointly commissioned to paint the great retable still in Valencia cathedral. The styles of both masters are distinguished by clarity of composition, a taste for static poses and attitudes, and an appreciation of architecture, less for the sake of the prolific ornamental detail, of which other painters of the period were so fond, than for the balance of masses. In the scenes of this retable, taken from the life of the Virgin, their debt to Leonardo is very obvious. Although the styles of the two painters have much in common, Yáñez's manner is distinguished by the greater monumentality of his figures. Llanos appears to be more addicted to the emotional gesture and the troubled expression. After 1513, the two artists worked independently, Yáñez producing the notable St. Catharine in the Prado, the Epiphany and Pietà of Cuenca cathedral, painted in 1531, and the Last Judgment in the March collection in Mallorca. Together, Yáñez and Llanos exerted a widespread influence on the schools of Murcia and Valencia.

Unlike fifteenth-century art, Catalan painting of this period, that is, of the first quarter of the sixteenth century, did not revolve about a group of exceptional personalities. Individual masters, mostly foreigners, produced work of some interest in different centers throughout the province, particularly in Gerona, Tarragona, and Barcelona.

The most eminent of these artists was Ayne Bru, a painter of German origin, to whom we owe the magnificent Martyrdom of St. Cucufate, preserved in the Museum of Catalan Art (Plate 121). This painting is remarkable for the sensuous opulence of the modeling, which is rich in tactile qualities and suggestive of the style of Leonardo. Gerona was the home of a very gifted painter known as Juan de Borgoña (of Burgundy). His work also appears in Valencia, and his art, with its wealth of forms and colors, was known along the entire Mediterranean coast of Spain.

ECLECTICISM

About the year 1500 a number of talented painters were at work in the principal cities of southern and central Spain. Their art is often eclectic, comprising both Northern and Italian elements, with the balance weighted somewhat in favor of the latter. In Toledo, the first third of the sixteenth century is dominated by the personality of Juan de Borgoña. In 1495 he worked in Toledo cathedral, together with Pedro Berruguete. His painting is remarkable for its exquisite sensitivity, its balance, and a warm lyricism intolerant of all excess. There is evidence of early exposure to Florentine influences, together with hints of the Gothic, especially strong in the fall of the draperies. Luminous colors and the subtle organization of space are the distinguishing features of Juan de Borgoña's magnificent decorations in the chapter house of Toledo cathedral (1509–1511), in which the landscape plays such an important part (Plate 123). In addition to executing several retables in Toledo, the artist also completed the retable of the Cathedral of Avila, begun by Pedro Berruguete, which includes an exquisite Annunciation. In his studio work, which is rather voluminous, some of the more valuable qualities of the master tend to be neutralized.

During this same period some outstanding paintings were being

121   Anye Bru. The Martyrdom of St. Cucufate. c. 1508. Museum of Catalan Art, Barcelona

produced in Seville by Alejo Fernández. In 1496 he is reported in Cordova, but soon afterward he moved to Seville, where he continued to live until his death in 1545. Strong in composition, Fernández was particularly skillful in handling his figures, which are distributed with imagination and judgment and modeled with unusual grace, as may be seen in his Epiphany in Seville cathedral. The cities of Sevilla and Saragossa possess important examples of his work, in particular the Virgin of the Navigators from the Alcázar of Seville, in which the sober and balanced composition and the nobility of form foreshadow Zurbarán.

During the second third of the sixteenth century, a number of Spanish painters fell heavily under the influence of Raphael. Typical in this respect, in Valencia, are the members of the Masip family: Vicente Masip and his son, Juan de Juanes. The work of the latter, mostly later than 1550, is distinguished by a certain formalistic elaboration of the directions taken by his father, and is by no means lacking in grace or skill. Juan de Juanes was the creator of a group of models of Spanish piety. His work is harmonious, rhythmically transparent, and well designed. These characteristics are particularly evident in his more popular compositions, such as the Holy Family in the Academy of San Fernando, the Redeemer in the Valencia Museum, and the Last Supper in the Prado Museum. His father's most important achievement is the retable in Segorbe cathedral, painted about 1530.

In Seville, the second third of the sixteenth century also witnessed the introduction of a style of painting that reflected the ascendancy of Raphael. In this center, the most important artists of the period were undoubtedly of Northern origin: the Dutchman Fernando Esturmio (Storm), and the Fleming Pedro de Campaña (Kempener). The latter, the more gifted of the two, was born in Brussels in 1503. He was trained in Italy, but in 1537 he is known to have been employed in the Cathedral of Seville. Shortly before 1563 he returned to his native country. The style of this master includes elements derived from Michelangelo, but these are offset by original

122   Alonso Sánchez Coello. Philip II. The Prado, Madrid

229

plastic qualities and a sense of drama. One of Campaña's key works is the Descent from the Cross (1547) in Seville cathedral, a painting that anticipates the Baroque of Rubens and was much admired by other Spanish artists, particularly Murillo (Plate 119). Campaña had a more amiable and genuinely Raphaelesque side, evident in the altarpiece of the Marshal's Chapel in Seville cathedral, which he was commissioned to paint in 1555. His progress toward the Baroque and his interest in the rendering of light are revealed in his admirable Adoration of the Magi, which was painted in 1557 (church of Santa Ana, Seville).

There is no space to mention all the numerous artists working in Spain at this time, but we must refer, however briefly, to the paintings of that sculptor of genius, Alonso Berruguete, in particular to his Nativity in the Valladolid Museum, and to the work of Pedro Machuca, an extraordinary artist whose architectural achievements have already been noted.

Luis de Morales (called El Divino), born in 1510, was a distinctly original personality. The distinctive features of his style—a painstaking technique inherited from the Flemish masters, and elongated forms that foreshadow the art of El Greco—are especially evident in the works of his final period. Morales painted numerous versions of the Virgin and Child, sometimes with the infant St. John, and touching visions inspired by the theme "Ecce Homo," which are among his most popular works (Plate 120). Sensitivity to content and concentration on the sacred drama are the chief characteristics of this typical representative of Spanish asceticism.

The third quarter of the sixteenth century brought a strong desire for innovation. This coincided with the infiltration of Mannerism, openly introduced by the Italian painters who decorated the Escorial, and a renewed interest in the Venetians, particularly in their colors. The painter who best represents these tendencies is Juan Fernández Navarrete, called "the Mute" because of the affliction from which he had suffered since boyhood. After a "short" stay in Italy, where he

123   Juan de Borgoña. Detail of the decoration in the chapter house of the Cathedral of Toledo. 1509–1511

had contact with Titian's studio, he started work in the Escorial in about 1568. Thanks to the forcefulness of the image, his realistic and merciless version of the Martyrdom of St. James (1571) is one of his best known works, but his Adoration of the Magi (1575), also in the Escorial, better reveals his painterly preoccupation with light, chiaroscuro, and color. Navarrete died in Toledo in 1579.

PORTRAIT PAINTING

The art of the second half of the sixteenth century was by no means exclusively religious. Portrait painting also flourished. The Dutch portraitist Anthonis Mor (1519?–1576) was followed by his pupil Alonso Sánchez Coello (1531/32–1588), who gave a decided impetus to this genre with work of the caliber of his portraits of Philip II (Plate 122) and the royal children Don Carlos and Isabella Clara Eugenia (Prado Museum). This artist has rightly been praised for his humanity, which, in its intimate relationship to plastic values, makes him the direct precursor of Velázquez portraits. The preoccupation with tactile qualities and the convincing representation of materials, characteristic of Sánchez Coello, is even more noticeable in the work of his pupil and successor Juan Pantoja de la Cruz (1551–1609). In his somewhat hieratic portraits, the character of the subject is of less interest than the verisimilitude of jewels, lace, silks, brocades, and nielloed armor. Pantoja, like Sánchez Coello, painted religious subjects as well as portraits, and in this genre he worked with greater freedom, achieving a more truly pictorial effect. He was also absorbed in the problems of dark and light, as revealed in his Resurrection (1605), now in the Hospital of Valladolid.

The last quarter of the sixteenth century produced a variety of painters who, for all their interest, are typical transitional figures, associated with a period of fluidity that was soon to crystallize in a new conception of painting. Prominent among these artists were Pablo

124   El Greco. The Assumption of the Virgin. 1577. Art Institute of Chicago

de Céspedes in Cordova, and, in Seville, Vasco de Pereira and Francisco Pacheco, the teacher and father-in-law of Velázquez, who in his latter years (1649) published an interesting treatise, *Art of Painting*.

EL GRECO

The great revolution that burst on the mediocrity of late sixteenth-century Spanish painting turned largely upon the genius of El Greco, Italian-trained under Venetian masters, yet a supreme individualist and the possessor of a technique as advanced and effective as any in Europe. There is something miraculous about the outcome of a career so full of internal contradictions and exposed to so many apparently conflicting influences. Born on the island of Crete in 1541, Domenicos Theotocopoulos must have begun to paint in the Byzantine icon tradition, which is discernible in much of his later work. Later, under the spell of Venice, he determined upon a very different course. In 1570 Giulio Clovio noted an encounter in Rome with "a young native of Candia, a pupil of Titian, who in my judgment seems to have a rare gift for painting." In fact, El Greco did develop his singular talents under Titian and Tintoretto and produced work of astonishing power even during these youthful years in Italy. Venetian influence is apparent in the portrait of Giovanni Battista Porta (National Gallery, Copenhagen), in the Healing of the Blind Man in the Dresden Pinakothek, and in other paintings. In Rome, in spite of his diatribes against him, El Greco learned much from Michelangelo, acknowledging, in particular, the grandeur of his conception of the human body, stressed by tensions that reveal a supernatural world.

News of the building of the Escorial, and the example of the Italian painters who went to Spain to work on its decoration, may have influenced El Greco's decision to seek new goals. His mysticism must have enabled him to identify himself with the Spanish ideals of the Golden Century more completely than with the sensuousness and literary themes of Italian art. In 1577 he was engaged in painting the great retable of Santo Domingo el Antiguo in Toledo, dominated by two great panels, The Trinity and The Assumption, now in museums in Madrid and Chicago (Plate 124). The El Greco of this period is still very restrained, concerned with closed forms, and able to invest his sacred themes with a sense of monumentality, while finding a means of self-expression in the tumultuous life of his colors.

El Greco's work is distinguished by a marked interest in human types, to which his success as a portrait painter must certainly be attributed. At the same time, this success is founded less on objectivity than on a talent for selecting models sympathetic to a conception of the world exalted by religious feeling. The culmination of his art is to be found in the paintings based on the Gospels and other sacred themes, such as the famous Espolio, painted in 1577–1579 (sacristy of Toledo cathedral). El Greco used the folds of robes and draperies to establish a rhythmical movement suggestive of the medieval style, but handled with the freedom of the Baroque. The reflections and textures of the fabrics are rendered with marvelous skill. In 1580–1582 he painted his striking version of the Martyrdom of St. Maurice (Escorial), a carefully studied composition with an original color scale of cold blues, yellows, greens, and violets. This work, commissioned by Philip II, failed to please the monarch and was refused.

Thereafter El Greco turned from a course that, if pursued, would have brought him greater wealth and honors. In 1586–1588 he executed one of his masterpieces, preserved in the church of Santo Tomé in Toledo, for which it was painted. This is the Burial of Count of Orgaz, a magnificent composition, based on a fourteenth-century legend, in which the artist expresses his disdain for externals and his interest in the "interior light" and the human form. In this picture the figures of knights and monks form a frieze beneath which two saints support the body of the count. The splendors of the heavenly realm are blazoned across the distant sky. The ascent to Heaven was a favorite subject of El Greco, a theme reiterated in his rhythms, chiaroscuro, and color. In these paintings the mystical element is counterbalanced by a profoundly human interest in the earthly model. In this connection it is enough to note the portrait of Cardinal Fernando Niño de Guevara in the Metropolitan Museum of Art, New York, and the impressive St. Alphonsus (1603–1605) preserved in Illescas.

El Greco was interested in landscape less for the sake of its anecdotal value and natural beauty than for its spiritual qualities and the

atmosphere. This is the mood of his masterly View of Toledo (1603 to 1607), also in the Metropolitan Museum. The artist also had to satisfy a steady demand for pictures of the saints. He was therefore obliged to resort to the expedient of painting them in series, sometimes with the aid of assistants. In this way he produced numerous versions, closely similar or with certain variations, of his conception of St. Francis of Assisi, the repentant St. Peter, St. Jerome, Mary Magdalene, and so on. In his maturity he allowed freer rein to a personal tendency to distort and elongate his figures, as in the Assumption in San Vicente de Toledo (1607) and in the Opening of the Seventh Seal in the Metropolitan Museum (Plate 125). During his final period, this tendency was exaggerated and combined with a process of simplification and elimination of detail and a frequent indulgence in contortion. These qualities he brilliantly combined with the most sumptuous palette, as may be seen in the Laocoön in the National Gallery of Art, Washington D.C.

It seems probable that the artist accepted the assistance of collaborators in some of the series he painted in the final years of his life, but it is no less certain that he preserved until the very end that absolute mastery over his art so conspicuous in the superb Twelve Apostles in the Casa del Greco. Francisco Preboste and the painter's son, Jorge Manuel, were probably his principal collaborators, while Luis Tristán was the best of his pupils.

125   El Greco. Opening of the Seventh Seal. 1500. Metropolitan Museum of Art, New York

Chapter VI

The Baroque Style

For Spain the seventeenth century was a period of serious national decline. The colossal heritage of Philip II was too great a burden for the last feeble representatives of the royal house of Austria. In 1700, when Charles II died without an heir, the frail bonds that had held this vast empire together were broken forever. The ensuing war, fought for possession of the throne, brought moral and material ruin to large areas of Spain, especially along the Mediterranean coast. In fact, the country did not fully recover from this long period of chaos and misery until the middle of the eighteenth century. A similar instability is apparent in contemporary architecture, yet, strange as it may seem, this century and a half of political and economic disaster saw the rise of some of the greatest sculptors and painters Spain has ever produced.

ARCHITECTURE

In Spain the term Baroque does not have the same meaning as in Italy or in most of Europe. In the architecture of the Spanish Baroque the native streak of individualism is encountered in its starkest and most exuberant form. For this reason stylistic and chronological classification is unusually difficult. A purely ornamental factor, reflecting the influence exerted upon architecture by sculpture and the use of

126   Fernando Casas y Novoa. Façade of the Cathedral of Santiago de Compostela. c. 1740

large retables, too often intervenes. A certain Mudejar spirit lurks behind the classical façade, the Spanish temperament revealing itself in the handling of the materials, for example, in the frequent use of brick, and great whitewashed walls framed in contrasting stone.

In our brief survey of the architecture of the Spanish Baroque we shall include buildings erected or designed between 1600 and 1740. This was a period during which cathedrals, and churches of lesser importance, were constructed, and more ancient projects brought to completion. There was a proportionate increase in the amount of civil architecture. The urbanization of the centers of population, though modest, continued at a faster rate than during the previous century. The state intervened increasingly in the affairs of the people, with the result that the capital tended to flourish at the expense of the provinces.

The formulas applied by Herrera in the Escorial were sufficient to meet the needs of the first decades of the seventeenth century. The style of this period is severe and bare of decoration. Between 1650 and 1680 there emerged a handsome architecture of elaborately modeled surfaces. This gave rise, in about 1700, to the so-called Churrigueresque style (named after the Churriguera, a family of architects and decorators), in which the structural elements became mere props for sculptural ornament. This style, which coincided chronologically with the European Rococo, was, in fact, the more original and, in spite of its early appearance, produced work of greater interest.

Madrid, the capital of Spain after 1561, was the scene of a series of town-planning reforms, including the construction of the splendid Plaza Mayor, designed by Juan Gómez de Mora, who also designed the Cárcel de Corte, an Italianate palace with twin courts, and directed the reconstruction of the royal Alcazar. Francisco de Mora built the monumental pile of the Villa de Lerma, Juan de Tolosa the hospital of Medina del Campo, and Andrés Ruiz the magnificent College in Monforte de Lemos, while Sebastian de la Plaza replanned the university town of Alcalá de Henares, where he erected a number of beautiful buildings.

Some Spanish architects did little more than adapt famous models

127   Sacristy of the Carthusian monastery of Granada. c.1740

to their own purposes, as may be seen in the façade of Santa Cruz in Medina del Campo, an almost literal copy of the Gesú in Rome. This building also exerted an influence on the design of the cathedral of San Isidro in Madrid. Herrera the Younger, who prepared the plans for the Basilica del Pilar in Saragossa, Francisco Bautista, and Pedro de la Torre are apparently the authors of the domed structures characteristic of the architecture of Madrid during the second half of the seventeenth century. The distinguished prototype of these buildings, designed by Pedro de la Torre, is the chapel of San Isidro de Madrid, completed in 1669. Madrid Baroque culminates in the figure of Pedro de Ribera, an architect of eclectic temperament, who stylized certain already established forms, grafting onto them a variety of complex ornament. There is something of Herrera's spirit in his hermitage of La Virgen del Puerto and in his church at Montserrat. In the façades of the Hospicio and the Conde-Duque Barracks, on the other hand, the extravagance of the ornamentation borders on delirium.

In Andalusia and along the Mediterranean coast the influence of Italian architecture was very marked. In Seville, the Exchange is built entirely in the Herreran style. During the first half of the seventeenth century, most of the building in this area, including some work of real importance, was in the hands of Hernán Ruiz, Juan de Bustamante, and Miguel de Zumárraga. It must not be forgotten that Seville was the port of entry for the products of the American colonies, and hence the wealthiest city in Spain. As typical examples of the architecture of this period we might mention the churches of La Merced, now a museum, and El Sagrario. The architect that did most to shape the personality of the Andalusian Baroque was Alonso Cano, a versatile artist whose paintings and sculpture are discussed elsewhere. In 1664 he designed the great façade of Granada cathedral, which, with its vertical rhythms and vigorous contrasts between mass and space, opened a new and fruitful path, eagerly followed by many of his contemporaries. The classical simplicity of Cano's style contrasts strongly with the elaborate construction that flourished elsewhere in Andalusia, for

128 Ignacio Vergara. Portal of the Palace of the Marques de Dos Aguas, Valencia. c.1744

129   *Jaime Bort Meliá. Façade of the Cathedral of Murcia. c.1740*

example, in the west front of Jaén cathedral. In some cases the façades look like retables upon which tiers of coupled and free-standing columns, the orders introduced at random, and lavish sculptures and reliefs have been recklessly superimposed.

An important group of Andalusian architects managed to evade the classical discipline, preferring the use of traditional elements, particularly tiles. Such is the case with the graceful Hospital of Charity in Seville. Another of its Andalusian characteristics is the use of stucco as a decorative medium, both inside and out. In spite of the evidence of Italian influence, the decoration as a whole is clearly original in conception.

The famous university town of Salamanca, the most important center of the Plateresque, was slow to accept Baroque influence, but

244

eventually adopted the style with great enthusiasm. Its greatest monument is the immense diocesan seminary, La Clerecía, built mainly by Pedro de Matos from the plans of Juan Gómez de Mora. From the end of the seventeenth century Salamanca was the scene of much of the activity of the Churriguera, whose name gradually became identified with the ornamental excesses of the Spanish Baroque. The elder Churriguera, José Benito, produced a masterpiece in the great retable of the church of San Esteban. Alberto Churriguera designed the broad and handsome Plaza Mayor in Salamanca, completed toward the middle of the eighteenth century.

During the second half of the seventeenth century, the Valencia region enjoyed a protracted period of economic prosperity, which is reflected in its contemporary architecture. These years saw the construction of churches as notable as Los Desamparados, a domed structure with an elliptical plan, San Miguel de los Reyes, El Carmen, and the parish church of Liria. In these buildings the brilliancy of the sculptural decoration is largely due to the adoption of the external form of the retable façade. In general, the Baroque architecture of the Mediterranean coast is characterized by the lavish use of ornament.

Like so many other Spanish monuments, the Romanesque Cathedral of Santiago de Compostela has suffered under the impact of successive changes of style. An extensive program of redecoration and reconstruction, carried out between 1649 and 1680, included the building of the Quintana porch, the dome, and the great belfry, all under the supervision of Peña de Toro. The Clock Tower was built by Domingo Andrade. The work of restoration continued until well into the eighteenth century, ending with the main façade, designed by Casas y Novoa (Plate 126). This façade, which dominates the skyline of the city, harmonizes perfectly with its flanking towers, and in its ornamental rhythms the art of the Plateresque appears reborn within a new stylistic mold. The Baroque elements of this impressive façade exerted a strong influence throughout Galicia, inspiring work in which the picturesque is rejected in favor of compositional balance.

Continuing across the north of Spain, our attention is claimed by a series of elegant towers in the region of La Rioja, particularly those of Santa Maria de la Redonda in Logroño and that of the Cathedral of Santo Domingo de la Calzada. In the Basque provinces, the domed

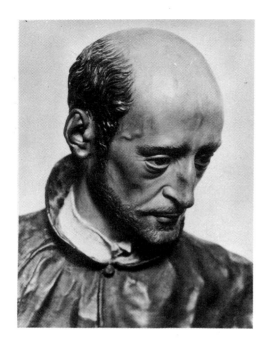

130 (Left) Juan Martinez Montañés. St. Francis of Borja. Seventeenth century. Polychrome wood. Museum of Fine Arts, Seville

131 (Right) Gregorio Fernández. Mater Dolorosa. Detail. Seventeenth century. Polychrome wood. National Museum of Religious Carvings, Valladolid

church of Loyola possesses a certain originality. In Catalonia, which, as we have noted, was passing through a long period of decline, the religious and civil architecture is characterized by great simplicity, occasionally, as in the church of Belén in Barcelona, reaching toward the fantasies of the Churrigueresque. The Baroque façade of the Cathedral of Gerona, with its monumental stairway, must certainly be considered spectacular in its effect.

We must now return to Andalusia and the Mediterranean coast in order to follow the swift course of its architectural transformation during the eighteenth century. Generally speaking, the local style continued to skirt the fringe of the severe structural idiom of the Herrera-Villanueva tradition, though enlivened by imaginative work that sometimes achieved the highest aesthetic level. The light and luminous Andalusian Baroque, which exerted such an important influence on Spanish-American architecture, inspired the construction of a great number of churches, public buildings, and palaces. The tortured

forms and elaborate stuccowork of the Andalusian style reach a climax in the chancel of La Victoria in Málaga, and in the justly famous sacristy of the Charterhouse of Granada (Plate 127). In the latter, the dramatic illumination of the Baroque, with its essential chiaroscuro, has been replaced with a filtered, evenly distributed light. The highly elaborate stuccoes assume qualities of the utmost beauty, and, in spite of their fundamentally Rococo inspiration, evoke distant memories of Islam. The last great figure of the southern Baroque was Leonardo de Figueroa, a fine architect and a decorator with a fertile imagination. His most mature works, the palace of San Telmo and the church of San Luis in Seville, completed in 1731, are highly characteristic of the Baroque architecture of southern Spain. In Seville, the Baroque cycle ends with the huge Tobacco Factory.

In Valencia, where a Rococo façade had been added to the cathedral by the German Conrad Rudolf early in the eighteenth century, we encounter an original form of art, best exemplified in the palace of the Marques de Dos Aguas (1740–1744). In this building the sculptural reliefs have an exaltation of rhythm and a material effervescence that foreshadow Art Nouveau (Plate 128). The magnificent west front of Murcia cathedral, with its harmonious and dynamic play of curves and contrasting solids and voids, was built by the Valencian Jaime Bort Meliá (died 1754). Work was begun in 1741 and carried to completion by the architect's pupils after his death (Plate 129). Though obviously influenced by the French Rococo, this façade remains profoundly Spanish, both in its decorative details and in the use of multiple planes.

POLYCHROMED SCULPTURE

As far as Spanish sculpture is concerned, the seventeenth century was the age of realism. The classical formulas of the Renaissance are

132   Francisco de Herrera the Elder. St. Catherine Appearing to the Prisoners. 1629. Bob Jones University, Greenville, South Carolina

133 *Pedro de Mena. Mary Magdalene. Seventeenth century. Polychrome wood. National Museum of Sculpture, Valladolid*

separated from the Baroque by the intrusion of a realistic art which aimed not only at close observation of the model, but also at the exact rendering of emotion. This is manifested in the idiosyncrasies of the style, in a preference for carving in wood, a warmer material than stone, and in the replacement of Renaissance polychromy with gilding and brilliantly imaginative lusters, touches that tend to intensify the verisimilitude of the image. This thirst for truth, and the prospect of economies, eventually led the religious sculptors to the "clothed effigy," only the head and extremities of which were carved by the artist himself. Before arriving at this extreme, they produced some marvelous and astonishingly vital figures with all the vigor of a portrait. This art was a more effective expression of popular piety than was painting. Nevertheless, the *pasos,* groups of sculpture which are carried in procession during Holy Week, are essentially pictorial in character.

During the seventeenth century, the great centers of Spanish sculpture were Valladolid, Madrid, Granada, and Seville. These schools may be distinguished by the greater pathos of the Castilian images, as compared with the ideal beauty sought by the sculptors of Andalusia. The school of Valladolid began with an important master, Gregorio Fernández (ca. 1566–1636), whose style owes less to Italy than it does to the North. His first known work is the recumbent Christ of the Capuchins (1605), commissioned by Philip III and now in El Pardo. Sober, refined, profoundly sensitive in his modeling, and restrained in his use of drama, Gregorio Fernández turned away from idealist aesthetics to portray the emotions of real life, suffering, agony, and death. His images of the Mater Dolorosa (Plate 131), which may have an antecedent in those of Juan de Juni, are designed to touch the hearts of the faithful, but at the same time satisfy the canons of plastic beauty. Fernández also carved retables, and his studio produced effigies for the Holy Week processions in Valladolid.

Overleaf 134 and 135:

(Left) José de Ribera. The Holy Family with St. Catherine. 1648. Metropolitan Museum of Art, New York. (Right) Juan de las Roelas. The Martyrdom of St. Andrew. c. 1612. Seville Museum

252

253

136 (Left) Francisco Salzillo. The Agony in the Garden. Eighteenth century. Polychrome wood. Salzillo Museum, Murcia

137 (Right) Narcisco Tomé. "El Transparente" in the Cathedral of Toledo. Eighteenth century

During the same years the Portuguese Manuel Pereyra (died 1667) was busy in Madrid. The Academia de San Fernando has a St. Bruno, rightly considered his masterpiece, in which the artist has captured both the spirit of the saint and the mood of a passing moment.

Toward the end of the sixteenth century, the central figure of the Andalusian school of religious sculptors was Vázquez the Elder. At the same time, the rise of realism is most closely linked with the work of the great artist Juan Martinez Montañés (1568–1649), known to his contemporaries as "the god of wood" and immensely famous even during his lifetime. Montañés learned his craft in Granada. His first known work, dating 1597, is the graceful—and pictorial—St. Christopher, in the church of El Salvador at Seville. Later, he evolved a

254

more strictly sculptural style, exemplified by the Christ of Mercy in Seville cathedral, a work in which the human blends with the divine. Montañés also created the Infant Jesus type, so highly esteemed in Andalusia. The foremost of his retables is that of San Isidoro del Campo at Santiponce, with splendid reliefs characterized by an remarkable humanization of the classical spirit. The artist carved a number of impressive heads for clothed effigies of the saints, including those of St. Ignatius and St. Francis de Borja now in the Museum of Fine Arts, Seville (Plate 130). Montañés exerted a widespread influence, both directly and through his pupils.

Alonso Cano (1601–1667) was an artist in whom restlessness lay concealed beneath a cloak of apparent serenity. His passion for beauty led him to create statues of the Virgin that have not been surpassed in this respect by any other Spanish artist. His sculpture had a profound influence not only in Seville, where he lived during his formative years, but also in Madrid and Granada. In the retable which he executed in 1629 for the church of Lebrija his personality appears to have set in its final mold. Gentleness and strength are joined in the figures of this admirable artist, whose most notable works include the St. Anthony in the Museum of Fine Arts, Granada, the Child Jesus with the Cross of the Cofradia de los Navarros in Madrid, and the marvelous Virgin in the sacristy of Granada cathedral.

Cano died in 1667. The most gifted of his pupils was undoubtedly Pedro de Mena, who was born in Granada in 1628 and began to work with Cano after the latter's arrival in that city in 1652. Pedro de Mena carried naturalism almost to excess, imposing the image as such upon the sculpture proper, as in the Mary Magdalene, preserved in the National Museum of Sculpture at Valladolid (Plate 133).

The panorama of realistic Spanish religious sculpture of the seventeenth century closes with a line of Andalusian sculptors, the Mora family, whose chief representative was José de Mora (1642–1724). The drama of his images is concentrated in its intimacy and always compatible with the purest beauty, as may be seen in his Virgin of Solitude

138   Juan Bautista Mayno. The Adoration of the Shepherds. c. 1620. Museum, Villaneuva y Geltru

in Santa Ana de Granada, or in the Mater Dolorosa of the convent of Maravillas in Madrid. In the work of José Risueño (1665–1732) Cano's influence mingles with certain Flemish traits, while the realism is partly neutralized by the intrusion of the Baroque.

During the final decades of the seventeenth century and through most of the eighteenth, there is repeated evidence of the workings of this Baroque influence, derived from Bernini and running counter to the realism and classical austerity of the trend whose course we have just defined. Andalusia was the region most affected. Sevilla was the home of Pedro Roldán, a sculptor born in Antequera about 1624. His principal achievement is the great retable of the Hospital of Charity, which was begun in 1670. Scenes like that of the Entombment reveal a decidedly pictorial approach to the design of a sculptural group. The artist's daughter, Luisa Roldán (1656–1704), known as "La Roldana," placed even greater stress on pictorialism, at the same time displaying a taste for anecdote compatible with a positive neatness in execution.

The most frankly Baroque of the eighteenth-century Spanish sculptors, particularly in his decorative scenography, is the Castilian Narciso Tomé, whose work is first mentioned in 1715, twenty-seven years before his death. His most famous achievement is El Transparente of the Cathedral of Toledo, completed in 1732 (Plate 137). This includes sculptured images in an ornamental framework that employs a type of parabolic arch not to be introduced systematically until modern times, about 1900, and figures suspended in space above compositions carved in relief.

The eighteenth century was the great age of the religious sculptors. These artists, active in all the cities of Spain, carved a multitude of altars and polychrome images in accordance with a general, distinctly Rococo formula designed to please the popular taste. Prominent among them, both for the quality of his work and the great fame he enjoyed during his lifetime, is Francisco Salzillo (1707–1783), the son of an Italian sculptor settled in Murcia and virtually self-taught.

139 Francisco Ribalta. The Last Supper. c.1610. Museum of Fine Arts, Valencia

259

Salzillo specialized in making figures for the Holy Week processions, to which he was attracted by a fondness for the spectacular and for displays of pathos. His best work is the processional group of the Agony in the Garden, which dates from 1754 and is preserved in the Salzillo Museum in Murcia (Plate 136). The humanization of sacred personages reaches a peak in the work of this sculptor, who was also the author of the Repentant St. Jerome in the same museum, which anticipates the realistic sculpture of the end of the nineteenth century in the care that the artist bestows on the rendering of detail. His most popular piece is undoubtedly his Nativity, inspired by those of Italy, but derived directly from the traditional Spanish crèche.

THE GOLDEN AGE OF PAINTING

The seventeenth century is in all respects the golden age of Spanish painting. Italian influence was largely rejected in favor of Mannerist formulas and a severe and noble style which used chiaroscuro not for the sake of a theatrical aestheticism, but to create a more urgent sense of drama. Though undoubtedly Baroque, this was a profoundly realistic art, preferring a broad visual synthesis, with a predominance of pictorial over tactile values, to the analytical approach of the sixteenth-century primitivists. Interest in the faithful reproduction of materials encouraged virtuosity. Artists grew more fastidious in their choice of colors and more intimately concerned with tonal values. Light served not only to lend brightness to external forms but acquired a transcendental function. Spatial values became more subtle and more numerous; tonal gradation gained in importance and the conventional mode of observation gradually gave way to one so penetrating that no other age or style has been able to equal it in truthfulness. It was, in fact, the great Spanish masters who guided European painting along the paths of naturalistic realism.

The new art remained faithful to the themes of the preceding century: pictures of religious subjects continued to predominate, but the patronage extended by the Hapsburgs to the more famous artists resulted in the execution of numerous royal portraits, as well as paintings of historical events and scenes from private and court life. In the

140   *Juan Sánchez-Cotán. Still Life. 1602. Fine Arts Gallery of San Diego*

best work of this period a superb elegance of gesture and a psycho-
logical profundity are combined with a splendid harmony of tones
and colors. It is a style that strikes a perfect balance between the graphic
and the pictorial, between the representation of detail and a suggestion
of the imperfections of human vision. The principal schools of this
period were those of Seville and Madrid, the latter enjoying the patronage of the court. Initially, there were other important schools at
Valencia, which maintained contact with Italy, and at Toledo, a
training center for painters who later worked elsewhere.

261

The first painter to abandon Mannerism for the new realistic style was Francisco Ribalta (1555–1628), a Catalan who, after receiving his early training in Toledo, spent the years of his maturity in Valencia. It is not known whether Ribalta was acquainted with the work of Caravaggio or whether he arrived independently at results parallel to those achieved by the Italian Tenebrists. At all events, his style is remarkable for its virile naturalism. The brushwork is increasingly bold and free, so different from the polished smoothness of the previous age. Ribalta sought expressiveness as well as beauty and accentuated the sculptural modeling of his forms by contrasting light and shade. Among his better known works are the Last Supper in the Valencia Museum (Plate 139) and the panels of the great altarpiece of Algemesí, painted in 1603; one of these, that depicting the martyrdom of St. James, suggests a connection between Ribalta and Navarrete. Juan Ribalta, Francisco's son, collaborated with his father, but died young, before his talents had fully bloomed.

José de Ribera

It is in the work of José de Ribera, however, that Tenebrism really triumphs. Ribera (1591–1652) was trained in Valencia, but in about 1616 he moved to Italy, settling in Naples. A clever draftsman and a master of composition, his numerous paintings are more varied than the legends concerning him might lead one to suppose. In his better work the dominant colors, browns and reds, contrast with cruel lighting, which sometimes appears to do violence to the forms. In Ribera highly refined execution and realistic modeling, particularly the marvelous flesh tints of his saints, are combined with a marked preference for dramatic themes, as may be seen in his St. Andrew, in the Prado Museum, or better in the painting of the martyrdom of the same saint, now in Budapest. His Crucifixion, in the collegiate church of Osuna, and his Martyrdom of St. Bartholomew (1630), in the Prado, are similar in intention and technique. A preference does not imply total exclusion, and there is evidence that Ribera was also a sumptuous colorist. His style evolved from an early preoccupation with "tenebrist" techniques, through a period of experiment with a silvery light, to a final stage characterized by warm and golden tones. One of his most

262

beautiful paintings is the Holy Family, in the Metropolitan Museum of Art, New York (Plate 134). Ribera also practiced engraving and his influence was considerable, both in Italy, where he lived in Naples when it was ruled by Spanish viceroys, and in Spain. Much of his work was intended for Spanish patrons and was an object of admiration as well as a stimulus to Spanish painters.

The school of Seville progressed rapidly from Renaissance classicism to the naturalism of the Baroque. Pacheco, to whom we have already referred in connection with the art of the late sixteenth century, was joined by other important masters, in particular Juan de las Roelas (ca. 1560–1625), one of whose monumental creations is the painting of St. James during the battle of Clavijo (Seville cathedral), dating from 1609, though even this is surpassed by the magnificent Martyrdom of St. Andrew, in the Seville Museum, a composition in which the painter's interest in naturalism and his rejection of formalistic representation are revealed in the vitality of the details (Plate 135). The figures in the lower part of the picture are especially fine. The spatial values are rendered with visual fidelity.

Another important member of the school of Seville was Francisco de Herrera the Elder (1576?–1656), whose violent technique was more daring than anything achieved by his colleagues. He excelled in depicting character. Typical of Herrera's work are the series of scenes from the life of St. Bonaventure (now owned by the Prado Museum and Bob Jones University, Greenville, South Carolina) painted in 1628 (Plate 132), and the Apotheosis of St. Hermengild, in the Seville Museum.

The Toledan school followed a course parallel to the one we have just described. It is easy to understand that around 1600 the dominant influence in Toledo should have been that of El Greco. The link with the master was strongest in the distinguished painter Luis Tristán (1586?–1624), who stressed the Tenebrist aspects of some of El Greco's work. Tristán's development was interrupted by his premature death, but not before he had completed work of such merit as the altarpiece in Yepes (1616) and that of Santa Clara de Toledo which was finished in 1623.

Another artist to receive his training in Toledo was the Murcian Pedro Orrente (ca. 1570–1645), who, in his youth, was a friend of

El Greco's son, but whose art holds closely to the course set by Bassano and Ribalta. Chiaroscuro is the principal element of his style, particularly in the paintings of his maturity. For the greater part of his life Orrente lived in Valencia and, in fact, became a member of the Valencian school. He painted numerous Biblical scenes in which the landscapes have a certain importance. These are dominated by the brownish and reddish tones popularized by Ribalta.

Fray Juan Bautista Maino (1578–1649), who was trained in the studios of Toledo, became the drawing master of Philip IV. He stands apart from his colleagues in resisting the general predilection for dark settings with the light coming from a single or one principal source. The transparency of his colors and the brightness of his tones are combined with a very individual sense of space in which something of the late sixteenth century goes hand in hand with a love of realistic detail typical of the new age. Two of Maino's works that claim attention are the Adoration of the Shepherds, in the Villanueva Museum (Plate 138), and the Pentecost, in the Toledo Museum.

Fray Juan Sánchez-Cotán (1560–1627), a native of La Mancha, also studied at Toledo. In his *bodegones,* or still lifes of food, remarkable for their purity of form and subtle balance, the light has a diaphanous quality similar to that achieved by Maino. His best-known still life is that in the Fine Arts Gallery of San Diego, California (Plate 140).

An interesting part in the transition from classicism to naturalism was also played by the so-called second-generation Italians, descendants of the artists summoned by Philip II to work on the Escorial. One of the foremost of these was Eugenio Caxés (ca. 1577–1634), a native of Madrid. Though his early work still reflects the Italianizing tendencies of his father, his painting of the Virgin and St.John before Christ in the church of Don Juan de Alarcón, Madrid, is thoroughly Spanish in character. Another artist with a similar background was Vicente Carducho (ca. 1576–1638), court favorite until the arrival of Velázquez. His work includes a great series of canvases, illustrating the history of the Carthusian Order, begun in 1626 and destined for the church of Paular. Carducho, well known for his book *Dialogues on Painting,* had numerous pupils, the most noteworthy being Francisco Collantes and Francisco Ricci.

Velázquez

The culmination of Spanish seventeenth-century painting, and one of
the climaxes of world art in general, is reached in the work of Diego
Rodriguez de Silva y Velázquez (1599–1660), an artist whose mastery
of space and light was admirably served by an impeccable technique.
Born in Seville, he received his first lessons from the daring Francisco

*141   Diego Velázquez. Christ at Emmaus. c. 1619. Metropolitan Museum of
Art, New York*

de Herrera the Elder, but soon became apprenticed to Pacheco, with whom he worked for five years, eventually marrying his daughter. In his writings Pacheco recalls how Velázquez was always extremely exacting in his technique and eager to work directly from life, preferring figure studies and genre scenes. Even the earliest works of the master are characterized by relatively dense impasto, objectivity of vision, restraint in the use of color, mainly ochers and browns, and simplicity and naturalness of conception. The Old Woman Frying Eggs (Edinburgh) and Christ in the House of Mary and Martha, in the National Gallery, London, and Christ at Emmaus, in the Metropolitan Museum of Art, New York (Plate 141), all belong to this early period. Among the portraits which Velázquez painted about this time are the admirable, vigorous, and thoroughly typical studies of Sor Francisca Jerónima de la Fuente. Almost all these paintings are executed in a Tenebrist manner which utilizes only the tonal organization characteristic of that style without conceding unwarranted importance to contrasts of light and dark.

In 1623, at the instigation of his father-in-law Pacheco and profiting from the fact that the king's minister, the powerful Count-Duke of Olivares, was a native of Seville and protector of his fellow townsmen, Velázquez went to Madrid and was presented at court. There he painted a portrait of Philip IV which so pleased the monarch that he enlisted Velázquez in his own service, granting him an official position in the palace. In this way the artist was able to familiarize himself with the magnificent royal collection. Thenceforth Velázquez became official portraitist to the royal family and the higher nobility. Between 1623 and 1629 he painted a number of portraits in which gray backgrounds of extreme sensitivity mark his liberation from the Tenebrist formula. The Topers (Prado), in which the artist burlesques the hallowed classical theme of the triumph of Bacchus, also dates from this period. In 1629 he went to Italy, where he remained for a year and a half, painting, among other things, the magnificent Forge of Vulcan, now in the Prado. On his return to the court of Madrid, he completed a Crucifixion of unparalleled serenity and simplicity.

The art of Velázquez developed irresistibly in the direction of ever greater synthesis. He painted the reflection of light in forms and colors rather than the forms and colors themselves; his drawing, such is its perfection, appears to illuminate his figures and details from within. This precision of outline, this subtle blending of tones and colors, this intervention of atmosphere between the eye and its object do as much to define the style of the artist as his simple and profound respect for everything in nature. A free and comprehensive vision of all the elements of reality, men, things, landscape, and, not least, the spirit, blazes forth in one of the masterpieces of his middle period, the Surrender of Breda, which he painted to adorn the Hall of the Kings in the palace of Buen Retiro, Madrid. His portraits of the grandees of Philip IV and the Prince Baltasar Carlos, now in the Prado, were intended for the same purpose. During the years that followed, Velázquez concentrated on portraits and scenes of the chase; around 1645 he made most of his famous studies of madmen and buffoons, one of the most striking being Boy of Vallecas (Prado) with its marvelous distant landscape. In the work of this period browns and golden ochers and the blacks, pinks, and reds of the costumes stand out against silvery or lead-blue backgrounds. The magnificent Coronation of the Virgin (Prado) is one of the several religious paintings he also produced at about this time.

In 1649 Velázquez returned to Italy with instructions to purchase paintings for the royal collection. While there he executed the famous portrait of Pope Innocent X and another of his own servant and pupil, Juan de Pareja. He also painted the delicate views of the Villa Medici, which have been described, somewhat mistakenly, as impressionistic, though their splendid luminosity, freedom of execution, and unfaltering technical strength, which must have aroused the enthusiasm of the masters of the second half of the nineteenth century, undoubtedly point in the general direction of the Impressionist style.

During his final period, between 1651, the date of his return to Madrid, and 1660, the year of his death, Velázquez, with a resilience rare even among men of genius, produced work surpassing all he had done before. A series of portraits of princes and infantas, mostly conceived as harmonies of pink, white, red, and black, was followed (1656–1658) by the marvelous Rokeby Venus, in the National Gallery, London. To these same years belong two of the artist's greatest works: Las Meninas (the Maids of Honor) and The Tapestry Weavers. While the former (Plate 142) reaches out toward the metaphysical, transforming its human subjects into transcendental aspects of a moment eternalized by art, the latter captures the essence of movement by revolutionary means, with "sketchy" drawing and blurred forms. The cold light of the foreground, which bathes the actual spinners, is contrasted with the warmer and brighter atmosphere of the tapestry, in which their labor is reflected. Both paintings, however, are characterized by superb compositional balance, by the static beauty that Velázquez was able momentarily to impose on every form of reality that escapes and flows. On the other hand, the painter's interest in portraying light was not the result of a preoccupation with technique, an attitude foreign to the aesthetics and even the optics of the seventeenth century, but developed out of a profound, inner religiosity, which had always been part of the Spanish tradition and was now to find new and vigorous expression.

These works were followed by further admirable portraits, like that of Prince Felipe Próspero, that of the Infanta Margarita, and several of the old king. The artist's superhuman virtuosity, however, did have one negative result: a lack of true followers. In fact, apart from Pareja (died 1670), Francisco de Palacios (died 1676), and, above all, Juan Bautista Martínez del Mazo (died 1667), now credited with a number of works formerly attributed to his master, the painters of the Madrid school turned aside from the difficult path trodden by Velázquez, preferring the lower ground of the Baroque, a style of painting brought to Spain by Rubens.

Alonso Cano

An Andalusian by birth and training, Alonso Cano did most of his painting between 1638 and 1652, in Madrid and later in Granada. This part of his career was divided between the execution of altarpieces and the portrayal of religious scenes revealing the highest qualities of an artist in love with beauty. In his conception of painting, Cano, a great creator of types, stands somewhere between Zurbarán

142 Velázquez. "Las Meninas". Detail. 1656. The Prado, Madrid

and Murillo. His frequently rounded forms are softened by lively and harmonious, but never strident colors. Strong lighting and vigorous composition give his figures, almost always religious, their distinctive plasticity.

The most noteworthy of Cano's altarpieces are those in the church at Getafe (near Madrid), dating from 1645. From that time on, Cano's technique became increasingly pictorial, that is to say, increasingly Baroque, acquiring some of the subtleties he had previously ignored. Perhaps his most important painting is the Descent into Limbo (in the County Museum, Los Angeles), a strange, rather illustrative composition, anecdotal in the movement imparted to the figures, but including one of the rare, and one of the most beautiful female nudes in Spanish art (Plate 143). His sense of drama, finds its most intense expression in his Dead Christ Supported by the Angel, in the Prado. Cano's gifts as a landscape painter are apparent in a number of pictures with Biblical themes, for example, in his Christ and the Woman of Samaria, in which the lights and darks have a strongly naturalistic effect.

During his later years in Granada, Cano painted a number of other important works, like the Seven Mysteries of the Virgin, brilliantly colored canvases of monumental proportions painted between 1652 and 1664 for the main chapel of the cathedral. Cano's foremost achievement is undoubtedly the series of Immaculate Conceptions painted at various times in his career, including a particularly fine one in the Provincial Museum at Vitoria, and another in the oratory of Granada cathedral. Fate has not been kind to Cano's paintings; several of the best have been destroyed in revolutions and wars, notably the admirable St. Agnes from the State Museums, Berlin, the Immaculate Conception from the church of San Isidro, Madrid, and that formerly in the Magdeburg Museum.

Zurbarán

Born in 1598 in Estremadura, Francisco de Zurbarán received his training in Seville with the painter Diaz de Villanueva. In spite of his wholehearted adherence to the Andalusian school, he remained Estremaduran by temperament, superimposing a natural asceticism and a certain rustic simplicity on southern grace and elegance. Although completely faithful to his own emotions, in his naturalism and intense chiaroscuro Zurbarán clung to a certain archaism that made him the most restrained and purest of the artists of the Spanish Baroque. In 1616, only two years after entering Villanueva's studio, he produced work as important as the Immaculate Conception now in the Valdés collection at Bilbao. Shortly afterward he signed a contract to paint series of compositions for several of the monastic orders of Seville who were his most important patrons. The Mercedarians possesses a magnificent series of scenes from the life of San Pedro Nolasco (1629), in which the qualities of the artist are fully displayed. His White Friars, a favorite theme, reveal his skill in the handling of ivory tones and broad parallel folds, like the fluting on a column, where gold and yellow reflections gleam even in the shadows.

Another important series was painted for the Jeronymites of the monastery of Guadalupe (1638–1639). Here the mood varies from a vein of realism to visions of miracles and scenes of contemplation in which the mysticism of the great Estremaduran artist has mingled with his colors. Perhaps the finest of these scenes is the mystical House of Nazareth, in the Cleveland Museum (Plate 144).

Zurbarán was also a master of simple themes, solitary figures, static and somewhat tense, saints with their eyes raised to heaven, and genre paintings in which everyday objects are clothed in mystery, as in the Contini still life of 1633. His appreciation of earthly beauty was no less strong than his feeling for the ascetic, and he painted figures of saints, like the St. Casilda (ca. 1640), in which the gracefulness of his Andalusian models is lovingly portrayed. The religious and artistic strands of Zurbarán's nature are impressively interwoven in a picture known as The Painter Before Christ Crucified, in the Prado Museum. Here, without loss of unity, he idealizes Christ on the Cross while intensifying the realism of the portrait, for which perhaps he himself was the model.

After 1640, Zurbarán apparently experienced an inner crisis. The twenty-year struggle to maintain his artistic primacy in an alien city must have proved too great a strain. New painters, like Murillo, were catching the public eye, and, to some extent, the painter of the White Friars sought to soften his mood, turning toward a more human, but

272

at the same time more ordinary mode of expression, which eventually took possession of his art. Zurbarán's last known works date from 1661 and 1662, shortly before his death in Madrid.

Murillo

In Spanish painting, and within the Andalusian school to which he also belonged, Murillo represents the height of elegance and delicacy, and, it must be added, the greatest surrender to popular sentiment.

143   (Facing) Alonso Cano. The Descent into Limbo. c.1640. Los Angeles County Museum

144   Francisco de Zurbarán. The House of Nazareth. c.1645. Cleveland Museum of Art

274

His art was always at the service of his theme, and the theme, in turn, was relived with fervor. In the fervor, however, profundity was often ignored in favor of more brilliant, but aesthetically less satisfying qualities. Murillo was as sensitive to feminine beauty and the beauty of children as to the subtleties of color and tonal gradation made possible by the advanced technique of the Baroque. Lyrical rather than dramatic, Murillo was by no means unaware of the prevalence of social unrest, reflected in literature in the picaresque novel, and his whole approach to religious painting was based on a realistic point of view.

A journey to Madrid in about 1643 enabled Murillo to study the Venetian and Flemish paintings forming part of the royal collections. Otherwise, he remained permanently in Seville, his native city, and his life was a simple one, free of serious problems. By 1645 his style had hardened in its final mold, as may be seen in the paintings executed about this time for the Franciscans, with the first of those figures of rascals and beggars in which he was to specialize. This is the spirit, for example, of the Boys Eating Melon, in Munich (Plate 146), and the Boy, in the Louvre, which is a study in yellowish ochers and browns.

In 1646 he began an extensive series of paintings of sacred personages and saints, executed with ever-increasing fluency. In 1656 he painted the Vision of St. Anthony, in Seville cathedral, in which a leading role is played by a golden light. A certain tendency to sketchiness in some of the details foreshadows the art of Goya. Between 1665 and 1680 he executed the twenty paintings of the Capuchin series. Another important series was painted for the church of the Hospital

145 (Facing) Juan Carreño de Miranda. The Duke of Pastrana. c.1680. The Prado, Madrid

Overleaf 146 and 147:

(Left) Bartolomé Murillo. Boys Eating Melon. c.1650. Bavarian State Art Gallery, Munich. (Right) Juan de Valdés Leal. The Assumption of the Virgin. 1659. National Gallery of Art, Washington, D.C.

277

of Charity in 1670–1674. The delicacy of the lighting and color effects and the ability to create distinctly human types are the primary qualities of Murillo's art, which inspired a host of imitators and followers.

The more dramatic side of seventeenth-century Spanish painting is well represented by Juan de Valdés Leal (1622–1690). He tended to give expression to the pessimism of the Baroque, which, for all his religious idealism, he was sometimes unable to suppress and which inspired visions as theatrical as the two famous pictures in the church of the Hospital of Charity in Seville. Painted in 1672, these reflect all the macabre aspects of death, in compositions that reveal the influence of the allegorical engravers. Magnificent as they are, these two works have detracted from the artist's reputation, since they have attracted too much attention to the themes of his art and away from his qualities as a painter. Impetuous, dynamic, a bold colorist who experimented with the principles of defocusing, Valdés Leal was a forerunner of Romanticism. Trained in Cordova, he revealed a propensity for violence even in his earliest paintings. Between 1653 and 1654 he painted a cycle of compositions for the church of the Order of St. Clare at Carmona, including the Attack of the Saracens on the Convent (Seville Museum), in which his qualities are displayed to the full. Shortly afterward, he painted an altarpiece for the Carmelites of Cordova, with figures of the prophets remarkable for their grandeur. In 1656 he settled in Seville. He painted his Assumption of the Virgin now in the National Gallery, Washington, D.C., in 1659 (Plate 147), and in the following year the version of Christ Bearing the Cross, now in the Hispanic Society in New York, both among his more decidedly Baroque works.

In Valdés Leal we begin to detect the freedom of treatment that marks the approach of modern painting. Asymmetry is often encountered in these compositions, which also succeed in creating an appropriate "atmosphere." In the final years of his life, Valdés Leal continued to produce cycles of paintings for monasteries, churches, and philanthropic institutions, among them a series of scenes from the

148   Claudio Coello. Retable of the Sacristy of the Escorial. Detail. c.1690

279

life of St. Ignatius (1674–1676) for the Jesuits. After his death the leadership of the school of Seville passed more and more into the hands of the followers of Murillo, who were unable to stave off the decadence resulting from the exhaustion of the energies of the Baroque.

During the seventeenth century, the school of Madrid, lead by the inspired Velázquez and Cano, developed a number of other lesser, but still interesting painters. Fray Juan Ricci's (1600–1681), son of a painter from Bolonia, arrived in Spain to work on the decoration of the Escorial. His painting is remarkable for its monumentality, a quality apparent in his seated portrait of Fray Alonso de San Vítores (Burgos Museum). Another is Antonio Pereda (1608–1678), author of a number of noble religious paintings, such as the Immaculate Conception, in the Ponce Museum, Puerto Rico. Especially noteworthy are his allegorical compositions, like those entitled the Knight's Dream and Vanity, in the Academy, Madrid.

More important is the work of Juan Carreño de Miranda (1614 to 1685), born in Avilés and trained in Valladolid, who painted in Toledo and Madrid. Charles II, successor to Philip IV, viewed him with favor, and in 1669 he was made painter to the king. Although his religious paintings are of unusual quality, Carreño's main interest was painting portraits, the finest being that of the Duke of Pastrana now in the Prado (Plate 145) and those which he made of the Queen Mother, Mariana of Austria, and of Charles II.

Another gifted painter of this period was Francisco Ricci (1608 to 1685), brother of Fray Juan, who excelled both as a church decorator and as a theatrical designer. A spirited colorist, Ricci has affinities with Valdés Leal, so much so, in fact, that his Immaculate Conception, in the Cádiz Museum, was long attributed to Valdés Leal, the painter of macabre allegories.

Mateo Cerezo (ca. 1626–1666), a pupil of Carreño, was a gifted painter and a good colorist, qualities which also appear in the work of José Antolinez (1635–1675), a pupil of Francisco Ricci. In addition to these artists, we should mention Juan Antonio Escalante (1630 to 1670), a thoroughly Baroque painter, with an eye for the subtleties of color and light, and a daring draftsman. In 1667–1668 he executed a series of paintings for the Merced Calzada of Madrid, some of which are preserved in the Prado Museum.

This phase of Spanish painting ends with Claudio Coello (1642 to 1693), a pupil of Ricci and an artist with an extraordinary gift for veristic representation. Coello's Baroque complexity, however, is combined with a naturalistic interest in detail that sometimes detracts from the formal hierarchy of his composition, as in his painting of Charles II and his courtiers worshipping at the Sagrada Forma in the Escorial, now preserved in the sacristy of the monastery (Plate 148). A remarkable portraitist, he has bequeathed a number of pictures of Charles II in which the degeneracy of the last of the Hapsburgs is reflected without the least attempt at mitigation.

In addition to religious painting and portraiture, the Madrid school of the seventeenth century practiced the art of the *bodegón*, or still life, in all its forms. Landscape painting was relatively neglected, in spite of the advances made by Velázquez in this direction. Toward the end of the century there was a diminution in the creative vigor that had continued to keep Spanish painting at such a high level, even while the nation's political reverses and economic crises were making themselves felt with full force. There then began a period during which praise was reserved exclusively for foreign art. This attitude persisted for a good part of the eighteenth century.

The same Charles II brought to Madrid the Neapolitan artist Luca Giordano (1632–1705), who lived in Spain for ten years, between 1692 and 1702, his virtuosity earning him the nickname "Fa Presto." His more important works include the painted ceiling of the stairway in the monastery of the Escorial and that of the sacristy in Toledo cathedral.

Chapter VII

The Eighteenth Century and After

During the first half of the eighteenth century, the Bourbons, who had succeeded the Hapsburgs on the throne of Spain, entered upon their own program of construction. Relying chiefly on Italian architects, the new dynasty built and enlarged palaces, gardens, and pleasure houses, like El Pardo, La Granja, Riofrio, and Aranjuez, at the same time erecting the present Royal Palace in Madrid (Plate 149). Designed by Filippo Juvara in 1735, this palace was eventually built by J. Bautista Sacchetti during the second third of the century. It is a structure of imposing proportions, inspired by Bernini's design for the Louvre, but related in character to the Spanish alcazar, a combination palace-fortress.

The second half of the eighteenth century saw the rise of Neoclassicism, due largely to the uncovering of the ruins of Pompeii and Herculaneum in 1748. The tendency to codify beauty, in order to restrain the excesses of Baroque art, led to the organization of academies. They claimed the right to unify and control art, an endeavor which was at least partially successful for a certain time. The Royal Academy of St. Ferdinand of Madrid was established by Ferdinand VI in 1752. Soon afterward similar academies were founded in other cities of Spain.

In architecture, this period is dominated by two men: Ventura Rodríguez (1717–1785) and Juan de Villanueva (1739–1811), who were employed both by the Crown and by private clients. Their work

149   Royal Palace, Madrid. Eighteenth century

282

illustrates the transition between the traditional concepts of the Spanish Baroque and the new academic style.

Rodríguez served as palace architect until 1759. His first important commission was the church of San Marcos in Madrid, completed in 1753. This building is characterized by elliptical spaces and curved masses, derived from the work of Borromini. The masterpiece of this early phase of the architect's career was the remodeling and completion of the huge church of Nuestra Señora del Pilar in Saragossa, including the design of a sumptuous chapel for the altar of the Virgin. During his second phase, which was marked by a growing taste for the functional, Rodríguez built the monastery of the Philippine Augustinians in Valladolid and the Academy of Medicine in Barcelona. Later, after becoming a professor of architecture and member of the Royal Academy, Rodríguez slipped into a conscious academicism.

150   Juan de Villanueva. The Prado, Madrid. c.1787

His last important project was the façade of Pamplona cathedral (1783).

After studying in Rome, Juan de Villanueva worked on the Escorial as architect to the Jeronymites. There he won the confidence of the royal family, Charles III and the future Charles IV. In 1711 he built the Casa de Infantes, and, subsequently, various other small pleasure palaces. In the house which he built for the prince in El Pardo, in 1784, the use of walls of red brick framed in white stone foreshadows the grandiose structure erected in Madrid, starting in 1787, which was designed as a museum of natural history, but is now the Prado Museum (Plate 150). This building is characterized by a predominance of the horizontal axis, and by the lively contrast of the masses.

Among the founders of the Academy there was a sculptor whose work was still essentially Baroque. This was Luis Salvador Carmona (died 1767), a prolific artist whose desire to restore the predominance of beauty over expressiveness and feeling is apparent in all his work. In spite of the fondness of the Neoclassicists for unadorned marble, polychrome sculpture persisted for several decades. This late flowering of an art which was declining imperceptibly into a simple craft, largely as a result of an indifference to sculpture on the part of the ruling classes, was particularly conspicuous in the Mediterranean regions. Spanish Neoclassical sculpture was raised to a worthy level by the Catalan Damián Campeny (1771–1855), whose work is notable for its formal unity and linear grace, as evidenced in the beautiful Lucretia, in the Museum of Modern Art, Barcelona. Other sculptors, such as Antonio Solá and José Alvarez, carved some interesting monuments, following the lines laid down at the end of the eighteenth century by the decorators of the Paseo del Prado in Madrid.

PAINTING

The first of the Spanish Bourbons, Philip V, engaged a group of French artists to decorate the rooms of the new Royal Palace in the manner of Versailles. Among the more gifted of these painters from the other side of the Pyrenees were Michel Ange Houasse, Jean Ranc, and Louis Michel Van Loo, who introduced the mythological themes and profuse decoration then popular in France. In the second half of the eighteenth century, a number of painters of different origin arrived in Spain. The art they brought with them was on a higher plane and exerted a stronger influence on the course of Spanish painting. One such artist, Anton Raphael Mengs, came to Spain from Bohemia in 1761 and remained for ten years. His work is a synthesis of subtle Rococo elegance and the severity affected by the Neoclassicists; his talents as a draftsman and a refined colorist are undeniable. His more important commissions included portraits of Charles III and other members of the royal family (Prado).

Two distinguished Italian painters also spent long periods in Spain: Corrado Giacquinto, between 1753 and 1762, and Giovanni Battista Tiepolo, between 1762 and 1770. The former executed various murals and ceiling paintings in the Royal Palace at Madrid. Tiepolo was also employed in decorating this building, his most considerable contribution being the great composition for the throne room, painted in 1764. The manner of the Venetian school, with its allegories, personifications, and attributes, was thus placed at the service of the Spanish monarchy. Tiepolo's subsequent paintings for San Pascual del Aranjuez, now in the Prado, are remarkable for their delicate colors and lightness of touch. Tiepolo was assisted in this work by his sons, Domenico and Lorenzo; in spite of the superior quality of his art, he had less influence on Spanish painting than Giacquinto or Mengs.

Even at this time the Academy must have played an important part in controlling the course of Spanish painting. During the second half of the eighteenth century, its tenets, which included an obligatory visit to Rome, or least a fairly close acquaintance with Roman aesthetics, were embraced by a number of influential artists. These included the brothers González Velázquez, Luis (1715–1764) and Antonio (1729–1793), who decorated various Madrid churches with paintings full of light and harmony, and Luis Menéndez de Rivera (1716–1780), a specialist in intense and strikingly lit genre paintings in which the masses and chiaroscuro are skilfully combined. Some of the regional artists of the eighteenth century also deserve attention, notably the Catalan Antonio Viladomat (1678–1755), known for his carefully drawn and well-composed scenes from the lives of the saints, particularly the series dedicated to the life of St. Francis, in the Barcelona Museum. The Valencian Mariano Salvador Maella, though Tiepolo's assistant, modeled his portraits on those of Mengs.

The most important painter to follow in Mengs's footsteps, however, was the Saragossan Francisco Bayeu y Subias (1734–1795), Goya's brother-in-law and the author of some notable frescoes both in his native city and in Toledo, the Royal Palace of Madrid (Plate 151), and other royal residences. The same artist supervised the preparation of cartoons for the royal tapestry factory, which had been founded by Philip V, but was not finally organized until 1775. Together with Francisco Bayeu we should mention his brother Ramón (1746 to 1793), whose work was also directed along academic lines. With remarkable skill Luis Paret y Alcázar contributed to the restoration of the thematic element to its former importance, infusing it with new vitality by cultivating popular themes, scenes of everyday life set amid conventionally bucolic landscapes, in which, however, there are signs of a return to naturalism (Plate 152). The courtly elegance of the Rococo period, never very marked in Spanish painting, slid through Academicism into an art that might justifiably be called pre-Romantic. This transformation, which occurred in the second half of the eighteenth century, was, at least in part, the result of social changes, notably a change in royal taste, in favor of rooms more intimate than the great halls of the previous age, and easel paintings with which to decorate them.

Francisco Goya

A tremendous change in Spanish style and concepts of representational art was wrought by the gigantic personality of Francisco Goya. His long career and vast output embraced all the phases of the transition from the Rococo through Neoclassicism to Romanticism, and his subject matter was as varied as his techniques. Imbued with constant restlessness, and endowed with gifts equal to all the problems with which this restlessness might confront him, Goya was a master of both religious and genre painting, of naturalistic composition and portraiture no less than of the fantasies woven by his soaring imagination. Moreover, he handled fresco and oils, pen and burin with

151   Francisco Bayeu. Olympus. 1800. Sketch for a ceiling in the Royal Palace, Madrid. The Prado, Madrid

equal skill. He could appear amiable or indiscreet, daring or terrible; he could assume the role of the avenger of a people oppressed by armed invasion, or that of the most fastidious representative of an art bordering almost on decadence. In his work violence and finesse are reflected not only in theme, forms, color, and composition, but, above all, in technique, in the handling, which may be subtle and precious or rough and abrupt, so that the brush strokes speak for themselves, without being subordinated to the concrete representation of the details of figures and landscapes.

Francisco José de Goya y Lucientes (1746–1828) was born in Fuendetodos, near Saragossa, where he studied with José Luzán. Even his youthful work is full of power, individuality, and technical daring. Twice, in 1763 and 1766, he entered Academy competitions, but without success. Shortly afterward, he went to Italy, where he produced some interesting paintings, including two "sacrifices," then a popular theme. In 1771 he returned to Saragossa. In the following year he executed the fresco of the Triumph of the Virgin in Nuestra

Señora del Pilar, and in 1774 he completed one of his great decorative series, the murals of the Carthusian monastery of Aula Dei. After 1775 he remained in Madrid, painting a series of cartoons for the royal tapestry factory, the evolution of which, from the first somewhat hieratic compositions, like the Dance in the Manzanares River, to the later Crockery Seller, remarkable in its conception, vision, and chromatic harmonies, points to the gradual triumph of reality in the artist's work. The next year, on the occasion of his admission to the Academy, he painted the Crucifixion now in the Prado. The fresco on the theme of the queen of martyrs, which he executed in Nuestra Señora del Pilar under the direction of Francisco Bayeu, proved a source of dissension between the two artists, Goya rebelling against

152   Luis Paret. Charles III Dining Before the Court. 1800. The Prado, Madrid

the impositions of his brother-in-law. Shortly afterward he began his series of portraits of personages of the court, establishing relations with the dukes of Osuna and Alba.

In 1789, on the death of Charles III, his successor, Charles IV, appointed Goya painter to the royal chamber; the following year, as a result of an illness, the artist was afflicted with deafness. This isolation contributed to the intensification of the visionary powers, which, at least in Goya, were always compatible with a marked respect for external reality. About 1794 he painted his scenes of witchcraft, in which it is difficult to know what to admire most, the delicate colors and suggestive mistiness or the inspired thematic invention. In 1797 he published the first series of the *Caprices (Los Caprichos)*, etchings on satirical and fantastic themes. Two years later he was appointed first chamber painter. His reputation rose steadily in every direction, the chief accomplishment of this period being a series of portraits of nobles and intellectuals, such as Moratín, Meléndez Valdés, or Iriarte. In 1798 he executed another of his great murals: that of the hermitage of San Antonio de la Florida, a painting handled with extraordinary freedom, in which the religious subject is treated as if it were a genre scene (Plate 153). There soon followed the two "Majas," and the splendid group portrait of the family of Charles IV (1800), a harmony of golds, browns, reds, and yellows.

In 1808 Spain was invaded by the armies of Napoleon. Goya celebrated the deeds of the Spanish people in two famous canvases, The Second of May and The Executions of La Moncloa, and in a stunning series of etchings, *The Disasters of War*. Shortly afterward, he engraved the bullfighting series, a theme close to his heart. This period is full of typical Goyas: occupational scenes, satires, and portraits, including works as famous as the Majas on the Balcony (Plate 154). But the culmination of his genius is to be found in the paintings he made in about 1820 for himself in his country house, called the House of the Deaf Man (Plate 156), images of horror and brutality, from a Saturn devouring his sons to a witches' sabbath dominated by browns and blacks.

153   *Goya. Detail of a mural in San Antonio de la Florida, Madrid.* 1798

In 1824, for political reasons, he left Spain and went to Paris and Bordeaux, where he continued to produce admirable work. After a short visit to Madrid, he returned to Bordeaux, where he died in 1828, not before having painted that marvel of sensitiveness, The Milkmaid, a feminine form that in some ways anticipates Renoir. Goya exerted a broad influence, even during his lifetime, and had many gifted followers.

THE MINOR ARTS

During this lengthy period the minor arts followed two trends, which, though at one point they existed side by side, correspond in general terms to the styles of the seventeenth and eighteenth centuries. The seventeenth century saw the continuation of the Renaissance spirit, occasionally adulterated with Mudejar elements, particularly in the applied arts. During the eighteenth century, largely as a result of the change of dynasty and the accession of the Bourbons, the French manner gradually became popular, though the borrowings from France were almost always modified to suit the national temperament and taste. In goldsmith's work, the preference for robust, compact, architectural forms, typical of the second half of the sixteenth and seventeenth centuries, was succeeded by an interest in ornament, often overabundant, and in filigree.

The silversmiths of Cordova acquired a well-earned reputation for the good quality of their work. The Mediterranean coast also produced some excellent pieces, including the candelabra made in 1703 for the Cathedral of Palma, Majorca, by the Barcelona silversmith Juan Matons.

In the finest seventeenth-century earthenware, that produced at Talavera, with its classical distribution of green, blue, and yellow figures on a white ground, the Renaissance spirit is still predominant. Less expensive ceramics with hieratic figures reflecting the tradition of

154 Goya. The Majas on the Balcony. 1800. Metropolitan Museum of Art, New York

294

the Mudejar kilns of Manises and Paterna was produced at a number of other centers. During the eighteenth century Talavera ware was surpassed by that of Alcora, a ware with tiny figures and essentially Rococo rhythms.

The extent of the great process of evolution which occupied the period between the end of the sixteenth century and the epoch of Goya is well illustrated by the contrast between interior decoration and furniture. The monastic austerity of Philip II's apartments in the Escorial might be compared with the splendid *salons* of the Royal Palace, the appointments of the palaces of the princes, and other royal seats. At the same time, the adaptation of French taste did not proceed without some show of originality, for example, in the unusual combination of damasks, furniture, and ceramics. This essentially Rococo art is seen at its best in the so-called Salón de Gasparini in the Royal Palace, Madrid.

In artistic textiles the dominant influences were French and Italian. The silks of Lyons and Venice were held in high esteem at the Bourbon court, and this brought new life to the Spanish silk weavers, concentrated mainly along the Mediterranean coast. As for tapestries, the opportunities presented by the foundation of the royal factory in Madrid were seized upon by Mengs and other artists even during the second half of the eighteenth century. Some quite original, though technically simple tapestries were woven from cartoons prepared by Bayeu, Goya, and others.

During the period in question, the dualism between popular taste, with its Mudejar base, and the foreign-oriented predilections of the court persisted and even became more acute. The Neoclassical and Romantic periods, of which the former, with the inevitable influence of Pompeii, was the richer in masterpieces of the applied arts, were followed by a period of eclecticism and industrialization. Art Nouveau succeeded in instilling new vigor into the crafts, producing magnificent work in wrought iron, glass, and the precious metals, and conceding the applied arts a more important role in architecture and decoration.

155   Vicente López. Francisco Goya. 1800. The Prado, Madrid

LATER NINETEENTH-CENTURY DEVELOPMENTS

The consequences of the Industrial Revolution became gradually more obvious. In architecture, the trend was, above all, toward the functional, and the economic factor became increasingly important. The cities of Spain, particularly Madrid and Barcelona, grew at an accelerated pace. Municipal planning received more attention, and numerous parks, gardens, and monuments were designed. At the same time, a number of artistically ambitious buildings were conceived along the lines of the better architecture of the previous century. In Madrid, two of the more interesting are the Royal Theater, built by Custodio Moreno, and the Palace of Justice, completed in 1850 by Pascual y Colomer. The chief feature of these buildings is the application of archaeological research in ornamentation, even in construction. Barcelona has some notable structures of this kind, the Customs House, for instance, and the Plaza Real. In Spain, the nineteenth-century interest in historic styles, particularly the Gothic, found expression in a reappraisal of the Mudejar. Even in the third quarter of the century the use of brick and tile produced some attractive results. Equally typical of the period was the rush to restore ancient, generally medieval, monuments.

In sculpture, Realism triumphed over the Neoclassical and Romantic views, and with it came scrupulous modeling and anecdotal, sentimental, popular, and descriptive themes. The period is well represented in the work of Venancio Vallmitjana, Agustín Querol, and Mariano Benlliure. The latter, though he brought to his sculpture certain essentially pictorial values, possessed undeniable strength and skill.

Nineteenth-century painting followed a meandering course. The Academician Vicente López y Portaña (1772–1850), a good draftsman, was particularly gifted as a portraitist, developing, toward the

156 Goya. Witches' Sabbath. Detail. "Black Painting" from the artist's house, transferred to canvas. 1821–1822. The Prado, Madrid

296

end of his career, a Romantic feeling for light and color (Plate 155). Pure Romanticism is represented by two painters active in Madrid: Leonardo Alenza (1807–1845) and Eugenio Lucas y Padilla (1824 to 1870). The latter was actually a follower of Goya as far as subject matter is concerned, though he exaggerated certain aspects of the master's technique. His bullfighting scenes are particularly noteworthy. Landscape painting was largely the domain of Pérez Villaamil (1807–1854), who was influenced by the Scottish artist David Roberts. Both enjoyed painting evocative corners of Spain and famous monuments, though their sense of style is somewhat distorted by a distinctly Romantic chiaroscuro.

Specialization according to subject matter persisted for most of the nineteenth century. The Academy had defended grandiloquent themes and fictional reconstructions of the deeds of the Greeks and Romans. This was the source of so-called historical painting, in which this tendency is combined with realism and the Romantic interest in medieval subjects. This art, much favored in official competitions, lasted into the twentieth century, and its consequences are still by no means negligible. It was practiced by painters of considerable standing, like Eduardo Rosales (1836–1873), author of the Testament of Isabella of Castile, which, though not without theatrical aspects, is beautifully executed.

In Catalonia, the beginning of the nineteenth century saw a certain artistic resurgence which culminated in the work of Mariano Fortuny (1838–1874). Though his refinement is clearly apparent in some of the landscapes in the Museum of Modern Art, Barcelona, Fortuny wasted much of his talent, doubtless naturally oriented toward miniatures and fine detail, on small paintings, in which he attempted to revive the grace and charm of an idealized eighteenth century. The artist's most representative work is The Vicarage (Plate 157), preserved in the same museum. Fortuny also excelled in pictorial reportage, vibrating with action, and, though realistic, charged with Romantic energy. This is the style of his huge composition The Battle of Tetuan.

Fortuny had a considerable number of followers, who in general adhered to his technique and his preference for anecdotal and realistic themes.

ART NOUVEAU

About the turn of the century, the stylistic movement now known as Modernism (called Modernista in Spain) developed more or less simultaneously in various parts of Europe. In Spain, it was concentrated in Barcelona, around the magnetic personality of the architect Antonio Gaudí (1852–1926). Born in Reus, he completed his course of studies in the Catalan capital, and at an early date assisted in the design of Citadel Park. In 1878 he built the Casa Vicens in neo-Mudejar style, making full use of local skill in the handling of tile, wrought iron, and brick, and giving the details a studied quality that was to be distinctive not only of his personal style but of much of Catalan Art Nouveau.

Shortly thereafter, Gaudí became acquainted with the Count of Güell. This amazing Maecenas commissioned the architect to design a whole series of buildings, where he gave free rein to his bold imagination. The first (1885–1889) was the Palacio Güell, a structure characterized by the systematic use of hyperbolic forms and by sculptured, ornamental chimneys, one of the architect's most original inventions. From 1887 to 1893 he built the Bishop's Palace in Astorga (León) in a sterner style, which reappears in buildings like the college of Santa Teresa de Jesús in Barcelona. His most brilliant achievements date from the first decade of the twentieth century, a period during which he designed the highly original Güell Park, where the sloping columns of the porticoes, though inspired by the Gothic flying buttress, derive a new expressiveness from the novel handling of the materials. These years also saw the construction of the Casa Milá, one of his apartment houses, the undulating façade of which has aroused universal interest. Here the general conception and the perfection of detail are equally admirable. The use of wrought iron in the balconies and of color in the murals of the entrance hall is extremely effective and indicates the high level of the applied arts in contemporary Barcelona. The spiral chimneys and the warped surfaces of the mansard roof also help to give the building its unique character, in which an undoubted streak of the bizarre mingles with the beauty of an authentic work of art.

Another of Gaudí's important designs is the church of the Colonia Güell in Santa Coloma de Cervelló. Despite the fact that this building

157   *Mariano Fortuny. The Vicarage. 1900. Museum of Modern Art, Barcelona*

is unfinished, it is remarkable for its structural innovations and decoration.

At the same time, his greatest undertaking remains the church of the Sagrada Familia in Barcelona, with which he was entrusted in 1884 and to which he devoted most of his remaining time between 1910 and his death in 1926 (Plate 158). During these years he was only able to build the Nativity façade, with its four tall spires and a porch laden with naturalistic sculpture, partly by his own hand and partly by collaborators. He also built the unusual crypt and made a model of the complete church, together with partial models of columns, windows, doors, and other details. Work on the Sagrada Familia has now been resumed. The design exerted a strong influence in Barcelona and in other cities of the province, where some genuinely beautiful buildings are to be found. This influence is sometimes explicit, as in Garraf's Pavilion, but occasionally takes the form of an undefinable air of Art Nouveau.

Other important personalities also came to the fore during the last quarter of the nineteenth century, producing work contemporaneous with that of Gaudí. The chief of these architects was Doménech i Muntaner, designer of the Hospice de San Pablo and the Catalan Palace of Music in Barcelona. The latter is typical of Spanish Art Nouveau in the importance attributed to the decoration. Statues incorporated in the structure, colored-glass balustrades, tiles, wrought-iron work, and so on, help to give it a fantastic and literary character. Finally, Puig y Cadafalch, who is also well known as a scholar and art historian, built the Casa Amatller in Barcelona in a very personal neo-Gothic style.

The Spanish sculpture of about 1900 is particularly decorative and lyrical. The most important sculptor of the period was the Catalan José Llimona (1864–1934), the author of some fine monuments, generally based on the female form, in a naturalistic and nostalgic vein that contrasts sharply with the realism of the later nineteenth century. In Catalonia, a classicistic reaction against his art was initiated by José Clará (1878–1957). The most distinctive, however, was the Aragonese Pablo Gargallo (1881–1934), who was trained in Barcelona in the Art Nouveau manner and who later went to Paris, where he espoused Cubism. Generally speaking, the sculpture of this period, particularly in Castile, is characterized by a return to tradition, although some sculptors, as, for example, Victorio Macho and Nemesio Mogrobejo, have indulged in a certain intellectual schematization.

Spanish painting of the period reflects a conflict between opposing tendencies, with a few successful attempts at synthesis. The Valencian Joaquín Sorolla y Bastida (1863–1923) combined the Impressionist tradition with the narrative and anecdotal tastes of the second half of the nineteenth century. His small, rich-toned paintings and beach scenes, and his sketches are perhaps the best of a large body of work. During the latter part of his life, Sorolla painted a great series of compositions on regional themes and visions of Spain for the Hispanic

Society of America, New York, analogous to the musical images of Albéniz (Plate 160).

Ignacio Zuloaga (1870–1945) also enjoyed a European reputation. Zuloaga, a gifted colorist, was fascinated by the Spanish Baroque. He excelled in portraits projected against evocative landscape backgrounds.

All this activity was accompanied by the rise of a new school of landscape painting, which, without identifying itself completely with French Impressionism, derived from that movement a fair proportion of its principles and techniques. Aureliano de Beruete (1845–1912) sketched broad panoramas of Castile in which the dominant element is light; Darío de Regoyos y Valdés (1857–1913), a highly sensitive artist with a certain ingenuous streak, painted views of orchards, ports, and urban landscapes, convincing in their truthfulness and poetic feeling. In Barcelona, interest in Impressionism mingled with Art Nouveau in the philosophy of a group known as Dels Quatre Gats, dominated by the personalities of Ramón Casas Carbó (1866–1932), author of some beautiful interiors with figures and a very important gallery of portraits, and Isidro Nonell y Monturiol (1873–1911), who died before his genius had fully flowered. Nonell painted the drama of the poor, but instead of treating it in terms of anecdotal description and narrative composition he compressed it into visions of gypsies, with all the tinsel stripped away. Somber forms, almost devoid of detail, and a range of greens and browns are the essential features of his work. During his final period, he painted with more luminosity, giving greater prominence to the brush strokes.

Another Catalan artist was José Maria Sert y Badia (1874–1945), though his style is diametrically opposed to that of Casas and Nonell. His interest in the Venetian masters was derived from a period spent in Italy. Sert decorated the Palace of the League of Nations and many other public and private buildings, including the law courts and the town hall of Barcelona and the Waldorf Astoria in New York (Plate 161). His best known work is the decoration of the Cathedral of Vich.

158 Antonio Gaudí. La Sagrada Familia, Barcelona. Begun 1884

Picasso

The great personality of contemporary Spanish art is of Pablo Picasso (born 1881). Born in Málaga, Picasso received his training in Barcelona, where he became acquainted with the group Dels Quatre Gats before moving on to Paris in the early years of the century. Even by this time, Picasso had developed an art profoundly personal in its strength and intensity of color, producing work which, though it betrayed the influence of Toulouse-Lautrec, was still more clearly stamped with the characteristics of its creator. A very important phase in the artist's career is that associated with the use of the Pointillist technique, seen in paintings like La Nana in the Barcelona Museum of Modern Art. It appears that Picasso painted the important pictures of his "blue period" while still in Barcelona, though the phase lasted until 1904, a year or two after his arrival in Paris. There then followed the pink and black periods, and a bout of Cubism, which, in the years preceding the first World War, helped him to develop his powers of analysis and to achieve an increasingly intense schematization of form.

Although Picasso attached himself to the Paris school, the essence of his art marks the culmination of the Spanish predilection for rapid technique and simplification, clearly observable in the artists of the past, including those of the Middle Ages. With his unparalleled virtuosity, particularly as a draftsman, Picasso inaugurated some of the most virile forms of twentieth-century art, at the same time achieving a synthesis with certain aspects of the past (Plate 159). After his Cubist period, which yielded work as interesting as the landscape known as the Horta de Ebro and the portrait of Vollard, he developed an enthusiasm for Ingres and Neoclassicism, but soon returned to his former schematic style.

Since the twenties, Picasso's influence has been enormous. An important phase of his work is connected with the Spanish Civil War, which inspired dramatic images characterized by a vigorous expressionism, culminating in the Guernica painting. Like Goya, Picasso is

159   Picasso. Mrs. Canals. 1900. Museum of Modern Art, Barcelona

160 *(Left) Joaquín Sorolla. Penitents in Holy Week Procession. 1900. Mural in the Hispanic Society of America, New York*

161 *(Right) José Maria Sert. Swinging. 1900. Mural in the Hotel Waldorf Astoria, New York*

not merely a distinguished painter, but an artist in many media. In addition to his drawings, he has produced extensive series of engravings and ceramics. A recent set of paintings, modeled on "Las Meninas," is a tribute to Velázquez and the Spanish genius, though not lacking in the irony typical of the Picassian temperament.

Picasso stands at the close of one epoch and the opening of another. The Spanish contribution to the art of the twentieth century, made, at least until 1950, chiefly through Spanish members of the school of Paris, has undoubtedly been an important one. Without attempting a detailed analysis of Spanish art since 1900, we shall now glance quickly at the achievements of some of the more notable artists of the period.

During the late twenties, a new generation of Spanish architects eagerly adopted the principles of functionalism. One of the leaders of this movement was José Luis Sert (born 1901), the author of various

model buildings in Barcelona and the central figure of Dels Quatre Gats. Later, the construction of the University City in Madrid provided an opportunity to apply the new principles, though in this case they are discreetly tempered by a respect for tradition. For example, brick is used freely and with great effect.

Since the civil war, but especially since 1945, the new architecture has developed vigorously. In Madrid, some notable achievements, particularly in religious architecture, have been recorded by Miguel Fisac. In Barcelona, the work of the "Group R" claims attention. The College of Architects in Barcelona, designed by Javier Busquets, is a fine, modern building, the latest one to be decorated by Picasso, both inside and out.

In sculpture, the dominant personality of the heroic period of the Spanish avant-garde is that of Julio González (1876–1942). González worked in France, but his influence has been strongly felt in Spain, especially in recent years. In his abstract sculpture, Angel Ferrant (1891–1959) combines diverse materials with considerable constructional skill; his mobiles, though recalling Alexander Calder, are original in material and form. Other important sculptors are Eduardo Chillida (born 1924), whose austere work in forged iron has definite individuality, José Maria Subirachs (born 1927), a more liberal artist who combines different materials, applying stress on color and texture, Marcelo Martí, Plácido Fleitas, Martin Chirino, and others. Iron is the most popular medium in modern Spanish sculpture, doubtless due to the example of Pablo Gargallo and González.

In the years between the wars, or roughly between 1918 and 1945, several Spanish painters working in Paris achieved world-wide fame. In addition to the loyal Cubist Juan Gris (1887–1927), there is the great Joan Miró (born 1893), and the much-discussed Salvador Dalí (born 1904), whose stylistic development consists of a chain of varied and hazardous experiments. Miró, whose work has been much admired in the United States, as well as in France, gives absolute precedence to color. His compositions are vigorous and gay, full of humor

162 Joan Miró. Dancer Listening to Organ Music in a Gothic Cathedral. 1945. Collection Edna K. Allen

and original rhythms (Plate 162). After an early figurative period, full of such felicities as the famous Masía, in the Hemingway collection, he adopted a freer, semi-abstract style, influenced by the Parisian Surrealists. His sculpture and engraving are of the highest quality. In recent years Miró has worked in Spain.

Salvador Dalí went through a restless period of Surrealism, during which he treated his images as "handmade photographs" and practiced *trompe l'œil* and quasi academicism. Later, he became interested in Raphael, Tintoretto, and Vermeer. His latest style, which oscillates between realism and mysticism, is displayed in his recent historical paintings, such as that dedicated to Columbus, and the Homage to Fortuny, works in which the painter aims at a synthesis of the traditional and the avant-garde.

José Gutierrez Solana (1886–1945), whose influence is still alive in today's school of Madrid, made the Spanish style topical by emphasizing a taste for drama and bravura. Solana, whose style has literary overtones, painted genre scenes, urban landscapes, and bulls; all his work bears a tragic accent. His somber color scale, based on earthy tones and blood reds, and the expressive sternness of his drawing are perhaps more characteristic of his style than his insistence on a limited range of themes.

About 1940, the school of Madrid, and Benjamín Palencia (born 1902) in particular, began to produce some unusually attractive landscapes. Simplification, intensity of color, and a vibrantly lyrical naturalism are the distinguishing features of this art, essentially a synthesis of Fauvist elements and traditionalism. In addition to Palencia, we should single out Godofredo Ortega Muñoz (born 1905), whose work, more sober and severe in character, is notable for the subtle modulation of its earthy tones. The course set by this group was followed by numerous other painters, though many were to diverge along paths of their own, often under the influence of Picasso.

Between 1950 and 1960, Spanish painting underwent a profound change following the introduction of abstract art by Antonio Tápies (born 1923), an artist with a highly refined and personal color sense who paints in thick impasto, scratching and scraping the surface of his canvas to create the impression of a relief. A few years before, Tápies had begun to work with a strong feeling for experimentation, and after a period of figurative painting in which he sought for magical effects he turned naturally to abstraction. Tápies has had a strong influence on all modern Spanish painting, and his own work has been granted international recognition.

The artistic spirit of Spain remains alive in many other contemporary painters: Antonio Saura, Rafael Canogar, and Manolo Millares in Madrid, and Modesto Cuixart, Juan-José Tharrats, August Puig, and Román Vallés in Barcelona, and so on. The new movements have also flourished in provincial capitals such as Valencia, Cuenca, Santander, and elsewhere, without preventing the parallel development of figurative art. All this work is intense and dramatic. In contrast to Miró's colorism, it favors earthy tones, grays, and browns, thus establishing a link with the Spanish Tenebrists of the seventeenth century and the "black paintings" of Goya.

Since Art Nouveau, there has been much activity in the applied arts, which have passed through a series of phases and styles. The greatest achievements in this area have undoubtedly been the jewelry designed by Salvador Dalí, the ceramics of Picasso and Miró, and the work, in the same genre, of José Llorens Artigas, who collaborated with Miró on the UNESCO mural in Paris.

During the last ten years, Spanish artists have participated actively in international expositions, contests and competitions. Thus, whereas the prewar period was marked by a certain isolation from international trends, there now exists an intense desire for communication across frontiers and oceans. The more distinguished contemporary Spanish artists are now represented in museums throughout Europe and America.

Index

Photographic Credits

The publishers would like to express their thanks to Ampliaciones y Reproducciones MAS, Barcelona, for their cooperation in supplying photographs of works from Spanish churches and museums. For other pictures, thanks are due to the following (the numbers refer to plates):

Alinari, 94
Art Institute of Chicago, 81, 124
Bavarian State Art Gallery, Munich (photographed by Joachim Blauell), 146
Bob Jones University, 132
Boston Museum of Fine Arts, 46
Chanticleer Company, 162
Cincinatti Art Museum, 91
Cleveland Museum of Art, 144
The Cloisters, New York, 32
Fine Arts Gallery of San Diego, 140
Hispanic Society of America, New York, 120, 160
Los Angeles County Museum (photographed by George Brauer), 143
Metropolitan Museum of Art (photographed by Geoffrey Clements), 125, 134, 141
    and 154
Morgan Library, New York, 25
National Gallery of Art, Washington, D.C., 147
Toledo Museum of Art, 92
Victoria and Albert Museum, London (photographed by John Freeman), 87
Waldorf Astoria Hotel, New York, 161

For permission to reproduce the following from The Metropolitan Museum of Art, special credit is due the Rogers Fund 1956 (plate 125); Samuel D. Lee Fund 1934 (plate 134); Bequest of Benjamin Altman 1913 (plate 141); and Bequest of Mrs. H. O. Havemeyer 1929 (plate 154).

318